Understanding the School-to-Work Transition: An International Perspective

UNDERSTANDING THE SCHOOL-TO-WORK TRANSITION: AN INTERNATIONAL PERSPECTIVE

THOMAS LANGE
EDITOR

Nova Science Publishers, Inc.
Commack, New York

Editorial Production: Susan Boriotti
Office Manager: Annette Hellinger
Graphics: Frank Grucci and John T'Lustachowski
Information Editor: Tatiana Shohov
Book Production: Donna Dennis, Patrick Davin, Christine Mathosian, Tammy Sauter and Diane Sharp
Circulation: Maryanne Schmidt
Marketing/Sales: Cathy DeGregory

Library of Congress Cataloging-in-Publication Data
available upon request

ISBN 1- 56072-604-0

Copyright © 1998 by Nova Science Publishers, Inc.
 6080 Jericho Turnpike, Suite 207
 Commack, New York 11725
 Tele. 516-499-3103   Fax 516-499-3146
 e-mail: Novascience@earthlink.net
 e-mail: Novascil@aol.com
 Web Site: http://www.nexusworld.com/nova

Printed in the United States of America

CONTENTS

CONTRIBUTORS

Clara Aase Arnesen   Norwegian Institute for Studies in Research and Higher Education, Norway

Jane Baekken   Norwegian Institute for Studies in Research and Higher Education, Norway

Jörg Christoffel   Federal Office for Economic Development and Labour, Switzerland

Monica Curti   Federal Office for Economic Development and Labour, Switzerland

Diana DeLuca   Education Commission of the States, United States of America

Udo Kelle   University of Bremen, Germany

Thomas Lange   The Robert Gordon University, United Kingdom

Anders Nilsson   Lund University, Sweden

Kari Nyyssölä   University of Turku, Finland

Gary Pollock   Manchester Metropolitan University, United Kingdom

Ian Shuttleworth   Queen's University of Belfast, United Kingdom

A. S. R. van der Linden   University of Maastricht, The Netherlands

R. K. W. van der Velden   University of Maastricht, The Netherlands

Robin White   *Academy for Educational Development, United States*

Stefan Wolter   *Federal Office for Economic Development and Labour, Switzerland*

Jens Zinn   *University of Bremen, Germany*

ABOUT THE EDITOR

Thomas Lange is Professor of Economics and Director of the Centre for International Labour Market Studies (CILMS) at the Robert Gordon University, Aberdeen, Scotland. He also holds the position of Contract Professor of Managerial Economics at the Polytechnic University of Bucharest, Romania.

Professor Lange is one of Scotland's leading labour market analysts. He serves as an advisor on several government expert panels and holds various honorary fellow- and professorships across Eastern and Western Europe.

Professor Lange has published over 50 articles on economic policy and labour market analysis in academic journals. Recent book publications include 'Unemployment in Theory and Practice' [Edward Elgar Publishing, 1998], (with G. Pugh) 'The Economics of German Unification' [Edward Elgar Publishing, 1998], (with L. Clarke, J. R. Shackleton and S. Walsh) 'Training for Employment in Western Europe and the United States' [Edward Elgar Publishing, 1995] and (with J. R. Shackleton) 'The Political Economy of German Unification' [Berghahn Books Oxford, 1997]

CHAPTER 1

UNDERSTANDING THE SCHOOL-TO-WORK TRANSITION: AN INTRODUCTION

THOMAS LANGE

INTRODUCTION

Against a backcloth of 36 million people unemployed in OECD countries and rising international competition concerns over the creation and maintenance of workforce skills have never been higher amongst developed economies. Whilst the battle against high levels of joblessness continues rising trends in youth unemployment have become a particular concern amongst policy-makers and their advisers. In some countries the problem has developed so dramatically that a considerable number of young people are at risk of long-term marginalisation and social exclusion. As a consequence, an increasing number of public policy options have been explored and examined to aid young people from school and college into jobs, both at the national and international level. In commenting on the White Paper on growth, competitiveness and employment, for instance, the European Council in December 1994 outlined an action plan which emphasised goals for action by Member States and social partners. Particular issues of concern included the improvement of education and training systems for the young and the improvement of measures "to help those particularly hard-hit by unemployment, especially young people, older people, women and the unqualified" (Field 1995). The Organisation for Economic Co-operation and Development (OECD) adds: "Although more young people participate longer in education, with potential long-run pay-offs for them and society, as many as one-fifth leave school without the prerequisite knowledge, skills or qualifications required for jobs in today's economy" (OECD 1996). In a world where capital is mobile as never before, and where the nation state seems impotent in the face of economic change, the skills of its youngsters seems to be all a country has going for it if it wishes to maintain and improve its living standards into the next millennium.

However, youth unemployment is not just a 'youth problem'. Both employment prospects and unemployment probabilities of young people are highly responsive to the overall state of the labour market. Ineffective means of employing people, either immediately after school or during adult life, have often been attributed to market failure. It is argued that the market cannot provide the unemployed with sufficient financial resources to participate in training programmes or to offer employers financial incentives to take them on. In recent years, therefore, much emphasis was placed on training, work creation and counselling and guidance to combat market failure and to try and bring the unemployed back to work. Policies that attack the causes of high and persistent unemployment will also improve labour market outcomes for young people. The young unemployed, together with women, the elderly and ethnic minorities, have thus been a particular target group for such schemes and the 1980s and 1990s have seen a sheer explosion of evaluations of these measures (Lange 1995). Until recently, however, many studies on training and other active labour market policies have suffered from poor quality surveys and missing longitudinal data and results have often been inconclusive.

In an alternative attempt to analyse causes of youth unemployment some commentators have concentrated on policies and proposals which aim to improve the links between schooling, family background and employment (Furlong 1993). Sociologists in particular have studied the link between social disadvantage, parental involvement and school performance and have argued that the effects of poverty on school performance and, ultimately, employment prospects are far-reaching. The concern about wastage of talent and the call for free school choice[1] has been a driving force behind many educational reforms and it can be seen as reflecting issues of natural justice, as well as economic considerations. However, it has proved difficult to measure the contribution of the different aspects of home environment because of cumulative and over-lapping effects, exemplified in the complex relationship between material deprivation and the whole way of life of a family.

However, some commentators feel that the creation of social equity in education and training can only be maintained if public policy tackles the issue of gender-specific labour market segmentation. Women, it is argued, are a disadvantaged group in the labour market and require special attention by policy-makers. Most empirical evidence seems to support this request. A recent study on German participants in further training programmes has shown, for instance, that, *ceteris paribus*, women experience smaller wage growth upon completion of training programmes than their male counterparts (Georgellis and Lange 1997).

The transition, then, from school, college or unemployment status to work is a complex issue and attempts to find the ultimate solution to such problems as youth unemployment, underemployment and social deprivation are likely to be unsuccessful. Notwithstanding this sobering thought, however, there is an ongoing quest to improve the transitory path from joblessness and educational disadvantage to employment. This volume provides an important contribution to this task by highlighting proposals, policies and experiences with school-to-work transitions in a number of OECD countries.

---

[1] Complete freedom of choice is, of course, never really possible without encountering problems of uneconomic numbers of spare places in the system.

PLAN OF THE BOOK

This book attempts to synthesise contemporary research on school-to-work transitions from a number of different disciplines in the social sciences, including economics, industrial relations, sociology and education. It does this in a way which should be comprehensible to education and training practitioners, applied economists and sociologists, advanced undergraduate and postgraduate students in the aforementioned disciplines and civil servants concerned with education, training and employment issues.

Following this brief introduction, the book is structured into three main parts. Part I is concerned mainly with descriptive analyses and draws on recent experiences of the school-to-work transition, reform ideas, policy successes and failures in the United States, Sweden and Switzerland. Particular emphasis is placed on historical patterns and developments (United States), the role of private sector influence (Sweden) and different schooling systems (Switzerland).

Part II consists mainly of applied work and outlines the crucial role of, amongst other things, formal qualifications and on-the-job work experience in the United Kingdom, Germany and Norway. One chapter spreads the net more widely and undertakes a broader analysis to examine the link between formal qualifications and employment (UK), whilst the other two chapters focus on particular educational levels: vocational training (Germany) and higher education (Norway), respectively.

The final part of the book takes a closer look at the role education and training can play to overcome the problems of unemployment and social exclusion. These chapters highlight the social policy angle of education and training by drawing on empirical material from the Netherlands, Finland and Northern Ireland. Particular issues of concern include educational mismatch (the Netherlands), long-term marginalisation (Finland) and social exclusion on the grounds of economic, social and religious inequality (Northern Ireland).

ACKNOWLEDGEMENTS

The book is the outcome of a major international conference on the theme "Understanding the School-to-Work Transition", held on 16-17 June 1997 in Aberdeen, Scotland. The event received some generous financial support from a number of private and public sector organisations. Particular thanks are due to Aberdeen City Council, The Anglo-German Foundation for the Study of Industrial Society, Chevron Oil UK Ltd., Grampian Careers, Grampian Enterprise, Marathon Oil, Scottish Enterprise, The Scottish Office, Scottish Power Learning, Shell UK Exploration and Production and Skene House Aberdeen.

REFERENCES

Georgellis, Y. and Lange, T. (1997), "Further Training and Wage Growth in Germany, 1984-1992", *Scottish Journal of Political Economy*, vol. 44, no. 2, May, pp. 165-81.

Field, J. (1995), *Spicers European Union Policy Briefings: Employment Policy*, Chapter 5, Cartermill Publishing.

Furlong, A. (1993), *Schooling for Jobs*, Avebury Aldershot.

Lange, T. (1995), *Youth unemployment and school-to-work transition: a critical (cross-national) survey*, European Science Foundation Working Paper, September.

OECD (1996), "Countering the Risks of Labour-Market Exclusion", *The OECD Observer*, No. 202, October/November, pp.49-52.

PART I

SCHOOL-TO-WORK TRANSITION - A SYSTEMIC APPROACH

CHAPTER 2

SCHOOL-TO-WORK TRANSITION IN THE UNITED STATES: FORGING A SYSTEM FOR THE FUTURE FROM THE LESSONS OF THE PAST

DIANA DELUCA AND ROBIN WHITE

INTRODUCTION

The United States is arguably the only industrialised country in the world without a national, institutionalised system to help its young people navigate successfully between formal schooling and rewarding careers. This chapter examines *why* there is no such system in place, *how* academic and vocational education became disconnected in the United States, and *what* is now being done to ensure that all American students can make a smooth transition to the world of work, regardless of whether they enter the labour market with a high school diploma, a baccalaureate degree, or post-graduate credentials. Moving from a historical overview of the roots of the school-to work (STW) movement in the United States to a discussion of the critical elements of successful STW initiatives, this chapter will trace the emergence of a uniquely American system of workforce preparation.

Despite abundant documentation of the obstacles encountered by young people who attempt to move directly into the labour market after high school graduation (Barton 1991), previous responses to this issue were largely local and piecemeal. This lack of response was attributable, at least in part, to the prevailing tendency to view college admission as the *raison d'etre* for academic success in high school, and entry onto a career ladder as an almost automatic side benefit to the baccalaureate degree. The conventional belief that academic achievement leads to college and college, in turn, leads to upward mobility actually discouraged linkages between career preparation and academic subjects and left generations of young Americans to flounder in job markets that were often skeptical of their skills, knowledge, and readiness for work.

Even though statistics show that almost one-third of the students in the nation's four-year colleges and universities drop out during or after their freshman year (Bailey and

Merritt 1997) and only one-half ever complete a four-year degree (Gray 1996), educators and employers have been slow to acknowledge the special difficulties faced by members of this population as they attempt to transition from the campus to the workplace without additional credentials or career guidance information. While college graduates generally have easier access to career pathways, many return home while they struggle to find meaningful and relevant employment. For too many recent college graduates, initial forays into the labour market take the form of low-skill, low-wage jobs. In the Washington D.C. metropolitan area in 1996, almost one-third of the Domino's Pizza delivery drivers held baccalaureate degrees (Matthews 1997).

The absence of a national school-to-work system in the United States is neither an oversight nor a reflection of the priority placed on education and training by policy makers. This seeming omission is a predictable outgrowth of the American experiment in federalism and egalitarianism. While the School-to-Work Opportunities Act of 1994 (STWOA) highlights the importance of a coordinated, strategic response to the overlapping needs of young people, employers, K-12 educators, and post-secondary institutions, the statute does not call for the creation of a "one size fits all" federal programme. Instead, the STWOA seeks a balance between local autonomy and equal opportunity by offering states and local partnerships the flexibility needed to design systems that serve all students, build on existing efforts, and align national interests with the unique circumstances of a given geographic area.

FEDERALISM AND EGALITARIANISM: AN AMERICAN "PUSH-ME PULL-YOU"

"A citizen of the United States," observed Alexis de Tocqueville, "does not acquire his practical science and his positive notions from books; the instruction he has acquired may have prepared him for receiving those ideas, but it did not furnish them." Americans learned by doing, he said, and they were never so clear as when they were talking about things they knew firsthand (de Tocqueville 1945).

The America de Tocqueville visited in the early 1830s was very much a work in progress. It was a land that bred individualism - self reliance, as American writer Ralph Waldo Emerson was later to call it - and a basic distrust of authority.

This distrust is evident in the wording of the Constitution, which sets in place a watchdog judicial function and explicitly states that "the powers not delegated to the United States by the Constitution, nor prohibited by it to the States, are reserved to the States respectively, or to the people."[2] Anyone reading the U.S. Constitution looks in vain for references to education. This is one of the powers reserved to the states. All 50 states guarantee some variation of a "free public elementary and secondary education"[7] within their respective constitutions, yet the governance and delivery of public education are traditionally controlled by local communities and/or counties.

---

2. U.S. Constitution, art. X.

2. Connecticut Constitution, art. 8, sec. 1.

While many European countries have well-established national curricula and outcome tests, recent efforts to develop common academic standards for U.S. high school graduates have encountered skepticism and resistance, even when these standards are described as "voluntary". The objection in this case is not necessarily driven by the concept of standards (which many states have already developed), but by their sponsorship by the federal government.

In addition to federalism, however, the U.S. is also an experiment in egalitarianism that plays out as a commitment to a particular type of social mobility. The huddled masses who provided the waves of immigration that built the nation brought with them the hopes that their children would lead brighter, more rewarding lives. As the frontier shut down, closing with it the avenue of riches based on hard work alone, the key to that bright future became education. Opportunity and education became virtually synonymous. This belief endures today when parents start saving for college as soon as a child is born, when a state implements a tuition prepayment plan, or when the Clinton administration proposes tax credits for college tuition payments.

Even though lawsuits were sometimes needed to extend equal educational opportunities to women, minorities, the economically disadvantaged, and students with disabilities, the nation's public schools and post-secondary institutions are, at least ostensibly, among the most heterogeneous in the world. Nonetheless, there are lingering doubts about the extent to which equality of condition has actually taken root in American education.

THE SEPARATION BETWEEN ACADEMICS AND CAREER PREPARATION: A POPULIST'S DILEMMA

In its most basic sense, the history of American public education can be summarised as a continuing debate about whom to educate for what purpose. This tension, evident from the establishment of the nation's first public high schools in Boston, Massachusetts, and Hartford, Connecticut, in the 1630s, has yet to be confronted head on and addressed adequately in both policy and practice. Although the Declaration of Independence proclaims that all men are created equal, the educational programs offered to American students are anything but equal. The country gives lip service to educating all students to high standards but continues to sift vast numbers of students into vocational and general tracks that are characterised by low expectations, watered-down content, and inadequate preparation for work, further study, or productive citizenship. As one keen practitioner observed, the U.S. has long provided *schooling* to the masses and limited *education* to the few (Chance 1985, p. ii).

A clear division between academic and vocational education emerged as the 20th century began to unfold and schools responded by clustering students into tracks or "ability groups". In 1917, the Smith Hughes Act formalised the division of vocational and academic instruction, providing federal funds to support "agriculture, trades, home-making, and industry, as well as teacher training programs in these fields" (Rumpf 1997). Although the Smith Hughes Act can be seen as an appropriate response to the economic and labour market conditions of the time, it nonetheless legitimised the separation of students into classes on the basis of their post-secondary plans or aspirations. As additional vocational courses of study were introduced throughout the next 50 years, differentiated courses became commonplace. Algebra, trigonometry and calculus were featured in the academic track, while vocational students were offered consumer mathematics or remedial arithmetic.

The practice of tracking persists to this day, even though it flies ostensibly in the face of American beliefs about equal access to opportunities. In schools across the country, the more rigorous, prestigious curricula are usually reserved for the "college bound". These are the students who can be found in "honors" and "gifted and talented" classes. They will take the Scholastic Aptitude Test (or another college admissions exam) and can expect to find their places in the freshman class on one of the nation's 3,700+ campuses.

The other students - those destined to move directly into the workplace - are offered a variety of "general" or "vocational" courses, neither academically rigorous nor relevant to the contemporary workplace. For those deemed "not college material", the high school schedule is usually filled with unrelated courses and classes described by one critic as "a large buffet of scholastic junk food" (Mendel 1994). As a 1993 study by the Institute for Education and Employment noted:

> *"Generally speaking, employers do not see vocational high school programs as a prime source of skilled or even trainable workers. Indeed, the very fact of having participated in a vocational program often stigmatises workers in the eyes of employers" (Kosmahl Aring 1993).*

In the midst of continued debate about what kinds of education to offer to which students, the U.S. Department of Labor (DOL) added another complication by opting to channel additional federal funds to vocationally oriented education and training programs for economically disadvantaged individuals, out-of-school-youth, and at-risk students. The Comprehensive Employment and Training Act (CETA), enacted in 1973 to support classroom instruction, job training, and subsidised employment for economically disadvantaged adults and youth, fell into disfavour after acquiring a reputation for placing participants in "make work" jobs. The Job Training Partnership Act (JTPA), the legislative successor to CETA, increased private sector involvement in training decisions at the state and local level and specified the percentage of funds to be allocated to activities for in-school and out-of-school youth. The Job Corps, established by the Economic Opportunity Act of 1964 and subsequently folded into the JTPA, now offers classroom instruction, counselling, and job training to severely disadvantaged youth (aged 16-24) in 111 residential sites.

While it is difficult to argue with the statutory intent of helping needy populations move into jobs, all of these alternative education and training programs have been widely criticised for the use of minimum competency requirements, placements into unrelated, low-wage jobs, and emphasis on short-term job retention. Each of these initiatives contributed to the increasing polarization of academic instruction and vocational training and reinforced the political acceptability of tracking.

WORKFORCE PREPARATION IN THE UNITED STATES

Though predictable, the divisions and distinctions between vocational and academic tracks represent a radical departure from the apprenticeship concept that skilled artisans brought to America. Within the young nation, apprenticeships were used to provide training in the professions as well as the crafts. Lawyers, for example, frequently served apprenticeships before starting their practice.

With the establishment of private colleges, professional training moved into the classroom. Harvard College, the nation's first university, was established in 1636 to produce public leaders, particularly clergy for the new colonies. A comparable purpose attended the founding of William and Mary (in 1693) and Yale (in 1701). Similarly, medical training became more structured with the founding of Johns Hopkins University in 1897. Until then, most doctors in the U.S. had apprenticed in the offices of European-trained physicians.

Even today, the education and training sequences completed by the nation's physicians, attorneys, clergy, and teachers reflect the endurance of the apprenticeship model. Physicians, for example, are required to apply classroom knowledge in the health care setting before they are able to obtain licensure and board certification.

An American university was also the birthplace of cooperative education, which has since become a staple offering of vocational education programs at the secondary level. First introduced in 1906 in the engineering department at the University of Cincinnati, the basic coop concept of integrating work experience and educational curriculum was clearly a forerunner of the contemporary STW movement. Nonetheless, the translation of this concept to high school work-study programs, with watered-down curricular offerings and job placements that are only marginally (if at all) relevant to classroom instruction, tarnished its image and limited its viability as a pathway for "college-bound" students.

Another major development within the U.S. education system was the creation of the two-year college campus. Introduced at the end of the nineteenth century, junior colleges were designed to provide the first two years of a baccalaureate degree. By the end of World War II, a broader mission led to the evolution of the community college, which provides not only academic instruction but also career programs, workforce retraining, and community service.

Encouraged by the Carl Perkins Act Reauthorization in 1990, a number of innovative programs in various states integrate the A.S. degree into a coordinated Tech Prep career ladder or cluster that is sometimes called a 2+2 (or a 2+2+2 when a four-year campus is added). One purpose of the STWOA is to build these types of integrated, purposeful programs for all students, not just the fortunate few who have selected a technical field in which such sequences are available.

FORCES FOR BRIDGING THE DISCONNECT BETWEEN ACADEMIC AND VOCATIONAL EDUCATION

Although debate about the merits of STW as a reform strategy for all students still tends to get mired in the pernicious notion that academics and preparation for work are an "either/or" proposition, there are positive signs of change. Global economic realities, new research into how students learn, and a heightened focus on student achievement by policy makers, business leaders, parents, and educators have created a tremendous momentum for change within schools. While some still cling to an idealised memory of American schools as they never were, there are new and insistent voices demanding that American schools do a better job of educating the nation's children.

Enactment of the STWOA, along with Goals 2000 and the Improving America's Schools Act (the 1994 reauthorization of the Elementary and Secondary Education Act), followed more than a decade of highly visible efforts to "reform" and restructure American education at all levels. The 1983 publication of *A Nation at Risk,* the final report of the National Commission on Excellence in Education, is often identified as the catalyst for the current generation of reform movements. The Commission did not mince words in its assessment of the condition of public education in the United States.

"If an unfriendly foreign power had attempted to impose on America the mediocre educational performance that exists today, we might well have viewed it as an act of war. As it stands, we have allowed this to happen to ourselves...We have, in effect, been committing an act of unthinking unilateral educational disarmament." (National Commission on Excellence in Education 1983)

The Commission's report was a call to arms, mobilising parents, educators, business leaders, and policy makers. It awakened the American public from years of complacency about the supposed quality of the nation's schools and catapulted education to the top of policy agendas across the nation. A flurry of activity followed, but increases in student performance were modest at best.

Although more than 270 task forces and commissions were appointed in the states to address the educational failings highlighted in *A Nation at Risk,* "first-wave" reform efforts focused primarily on increasing the numbers or changing the inputs, i.e. increasing the number of Carnegie units and courses in specific subject areas (e.g., English and mathematics) required for graduation. A 1985 analysis of education reform efforts revealed that 43 states had increased their graduation requirements and another five were considering doing so. Almost as many states (37) had introduced new assessments and at least 20 had either increased college admission requirements or were considering such action. Smaller, but still significant numbers of states, had mandated additional instructional time and/or promotional or exit tests (Chance 1985, p. 113). However, the vast majority of these requirements were cast in terms of minimum performance, and students across the country responded with minimal levels of performance.

Despite heightened legislative activity and public interest, many observers were not surprised that this initial wave of education reform had limited impact on student achievement. In his aptly named book, *The Predictable Failure of School Reform*, Seymour Sarason summarises the initial wave of reform efforts as "we will do what we have been doing, or what we ought to be doing, only we will now do it better" (Sarason 1990). More of the same - more courses, more seat time, more didactic lectures, and more standardized, norm-referenced assessments - yielded exactly what one might expect: more disaffected students; continued employer and post-secondary complaints about the lack of readiness of the students who came to them; and greater disparity between educational "haves" and "have nots."

Clearly the policy makers who set out to "legislate learning" (Wise 1979) in the mid-1980s failed to anticipate a number of adverse side effects. The "more is better" approach diverted attention from "more basic reform in the structure and practice of schools" (Corbett and Wilson 1990). The prominence of new statewide testing mandates forced teachers to devote precious instructional time to test administration, and actually led to a narrowing of curricular content and course offerings (the proverbial "teaching to the test") in some locations (Corbett and Wilson 1990). Perhaps most damaging of all, these initial reforms overlooked the nation's sizeable pool of at-risk students. Already discouraged by their struggles to meet existing requirements, significant numbers of these students simply gave up and dropped out when the academic bar was raised.

By 1989, continued dissatisfaction with the academic achievements of American students and doubts about the results of "reforms" to date were strong enough to prompt an unprecedented response: an education summit convened by President Bush and attended by all of the nation's governors (including then-Arkansas Governor Bill Clinton). With President Bush asserting that the "American people are ready for radical reforms"[19], Summit participants announced a new commitment to educate all students to high standards. The National Education Goals, a year later by the President and the governors, reinforced this commitment and explicitly tied public education to preparation for work. The text of Goal Three outlines what schools are expected to do and when:

"By the year 2000, all students will leave grades 4, 8, and 12 having demonstrated mastery over challenging subject matter... and every school in America will ensure

---

[3] New York Times, October 1, 1989, sect. 4, pp. 1 & 22, cited in Cuban (1995, p.81).

that all students learn to use their minds well, so they may be prepared for responsible citizenship, further learning, and productive employment in our modern economy."
(National Education Goals Panel 1996).

The 1989 Education Summit can be seen as a demarcation point - a very public acknowledgment that bolder, broader strokes were needed. The focus began to shift from what and when students are taught to what, where, and how students learn. This time around, the targets were not just numbers. The targets were the very fabric of public education as most Americans have known it: hierarchical governance structures; the ways that schools organise time, space, staff, and resources; the practice of sorting or "tracking" students and assigning them to classes; the division or splintering knowledge into subjects; the presumption that most learning takes place in the classroom during the school day; and the policies established to award grades, credits, and Carnegie units as evidence of learning.

Another milestone was reached in June 1991, when the Secretary's Commission on Achieving Necessary Skills (SCANS) issued *What Work Requires of Schools: A SCANS Report for America 2000* (The Secretary's Commission on Achieving Necessary Skills 1992). Called together by the U.S. Department of Labor, the Commission was composed of educators, board of education members, representatives of education organisations, state government leaders, and executives of some of America's largest businesses and industries.

The report outlined five competencies and three foundation qualities that have come to be known as the SCANS skills:

COMPETENCIES: the ability to:
*   allocate time, money, materials, space, and staff;
*   work in teams, negotiate, work with others from diverse backgrounds;
*   acquire and evaluate data, organize and communicate information;
*   understand systems, including concepts of performance and improvement; and
*   work with technology.

and

FOUNDATION SKILLS: the ability to fulfill tasks of:
*   reading, writing, arithmetic, mathematics, speaking, and listening;
*   creative thinking, decision making, problem solving, knowing how to learn and reason; and
*   responsibility, self-esteem, self-management, sociability, and integrity

As the 1990s unfolded, it became fashionable to label almost any change in public education "systemic reform", but demonstrable changes in student achievement and the educational infrastructure continue to be few and far between. Many of these changes have taken the *reform du jour* approach, i.e. they have been short-term, limited in scope, or focused on a particular segment of education (e.g., high school or middle school), a stratified sample of the student population, or a specific subject/curriculum. While these project approaches could be part of a systemic reform effort, few have generated and sustained the energy needed to drive comprehensive reform and restructuring.

Regina Kyle (1995) defines systemic reform as "a philosophical base for transforming education and a process for guiding the changes needed in schooling at any point in time." Other scholars and observers have identified the following characteristics as critical indicators of systemic reform:

coherence;
alignment of structure, policies, and procedures;
clear goals and objectives (clarity of purpose);
authority commensurate with accountability;
emphasis on standards and outcomes instead of input measures;
commitment to higher achievement levels for all students; and
use of learner-centered, authentic, and/or applied approaches to instruction.

Measured against such stringent criteria, it is easy to see why most reforms fell short of their "systemic" plans. The STWOA offers a new catalyst for change, reflecting all of these critical elements of systemic reform in its statutory language. What remains unclear, however, is whether the STWOA will be able to transcend its perceived roots in vocational education to drive a broader reform agenda.

STW AS THE NEXUS OF REFORM: WHAT DO SUCCESSFUL SYSTEMS LOOK LIKE?

While the STWOA is the first national effort to link school-based learning and work-based learning in a systematic way, this statute and the STW legislation enacted in many states reflect the pioneering work of successful practitioners across the country. A number of schools and communities anticipated the current national interest in STW, launching their own programs and services to help young people move smoothly from secondary or post-secondary education into the labour market. The end result was a patchwork of programs, projects, and initiatives, each with its own funding streams, policies, and constituencies. Even though the autonomy of these predecessors now poses challenges to STW system builders, these programs and initiatives also offer a wealth of information about what works and why.

Research conducted by the Academy for Educational Development (AED), Jobs for the Future, the National Center for Research in Vocational Education, the Manpower Demonstration Research Corporation, and others has confirmed that common themes or programmatic elements can be found across various types of successful STW initiatives (e.g., programs that are work-based, school-based, or operated by community organisations). A 1995 AED study of 14 exemplary STW programs across the country identified 11 key characteristics or elements (Charner et al. 1995, 1996). Although no single site exhibited all 11 characteristics, the resulting list of elements illustrates the range of features present in successful STW initiatives. This list of elements should thus be viewed as a menu from which to choose rather than a recipe to be followed exactly. A brief description of each element is followed by an exploration of how it is being applied to or incorporated into the emerging state STW systems and their component local partnerships.

Executive Leadership

Successful STW programs rarely stand alone; they have the visible support of school administrators (i.e., principals and/or superintendents) and policy makers (i.e., members of the board of education). At the local, regional, and state levels, similar executive leadership and commitment are needed to build and sustain STW systems. Governors, commissioners of education, labour, and higher education, legislators, mayors, business executives, labour officials, and leaders of community-based organisations have to demonstrate a shared vision of STW and a willingness to take the steps necessary to achieve that vision. In some instances, these steps might require transfers of authority, statutory or regulatory waivers, or redirection of funding streams.

Instructional Leadership

The staff responsible for programme implementation and delivery - STW coordinators, teachers, counselors, and others - is innovative, adaptable, and willing to experiment with curriculum, pedagogy, classroom management, and staffing configurations. In state and local STW partnerships, the empowerment of key staff (in multiple agencies and institutions) can be seen as a functional equivalent to instructional leadership. Even though the commitment of key executives is critical during the early stages of system building, a hierarchical or top-down approach to decision-making is likely to be inefficient and counter-productive. Front-line staff who are asked to assume new roles and responsibilities, and to forge relationships that transcend existing jurisdictional boundaries, cannot move forward if they fear recriminations and have to obtain permission for each new step in the process.

Cross-Sector Collaboration

A hallmark of successful STW programs is the active participation of a wide range of partners: employers, K-12 educators, organised labour, community-based organisations, post-secondary institutions, social and health service providers, parents, and students. The STWOA explicitly recognises the importance of cross-sector collaboration at all levels. One of the explicit purposes of this statute is to promote the formation of local partnerships that are dedicated to linking the worlds of school and work. In order to qualify for the venture capital available under the STWOA, the architects of state STW systems must describe how they will obtain and sustain the active participation of employers, locally elected officials, secondary schools, post-secondary educational institutions, business associations, industrial extension centers, employees, labour organisations, teachers, related services personnel, students, parents, community-based organisations, Indian tribes, registered apprenticeship agencies, vocational education agencies, vocational student organisations, and human service agencies.[4]

Serving a wide range of students

Successful STW programs are inclusive rather than exclusive; they are designed to help all youth acquire the skills and knowledge needed to move from the classroom to the workplace, regardless of whether they plan to make the move after graduation from high school or a post-secondary institution.

With its egalitarian emphasis on *all students*, the STWOA is a dramatic departure from the categorical programs and grants of the past. The Act explicitly seeks "to help all students attain high academic and occupational standards", and to provide opportunities "for all students to participate in high quality work-based learning experiences."[5] State and local partnerships are required to offer all students equal access to the full range of programme components. For both state system builders and local partnerships, the real challenge inherent to serving all students is going to scale. Mustering the political will to make STW opportunities accessible to all students is only the first step; finding the resources to provide these opportunities to all students is a task of immense proportions.

Integration of Academic and Occupational Study

Curricula used in STW programs provide multiple points of connection between the classroom and the work site in order to integrate academic, occupational, and work readiness instruction, and link this instruction to work-based learning opportunities. The STWOA gives statutory recognition to the integration of academic and vocational learning, and the extent to which such integration is occurring is deemed a key indicator of progress in STW system building. The STW progress measures survey, developed collaboratively by the National School-to-Work Office, MPR Associates, the School-to-Work Learning and Information Center, and a task force of state grantees, asks for the number of secondary schools providing activities that integrate academic and vocational instruction as well as the number of students who participate in those activities. Local partnerships are also asked to identify the number of secondary schools linking integrated curricula with work-based learning experiences and the number of students participating in those experiences. Because the survey is completed annually by local STW partnerships across the country (and data are subsequently aggregated at the state and national levels), it will be relatively easy to track changes in the availability of

---

[4]. The School-to-Work Opportunities Act of 1994 (STWOA), Title II, sec. 203(b)(3).

[5]. Ibid., sec. 3(a)(7) and 3(a)(3).

integrated curricular offerings and the rates of student participation in activities that link integrated curricula with work-based learning.

Multiple Options for Work-based Learning

Students of all ages need opportunities to participate in developmentally appropriate task-oriented relationships with other students, adults in the community, and employers. Ideally, work-based learning takes the form of a progressively more challenging sequence of activities and experiences, but the sequence does not necessarily culminate in a highly structured apprenticeship for every student. The STWOA shines a new and intensive spotlight on work-based learning, identifying it as one of the three essential components of all STW programs. The statute lists the broad categories of activities that must be included in the work-based learning component, but it stops short of prescribing where, when, and how to offer these activities. The work-based learning component of STW programs must include: workplace mentoring; instruction in general workplace competencies; exposure to all aspects of an industry; and a planned programme of job training and work experiences that are coordinated with school-based learning, are relevant to students' career majors, and lead to the award of skill certificates.[6] State system builders and local partnerships are offered considerable latitude in the selection and implementation of appropriate menus of work-based learning activities, but the results of their efforts are tracked through the annual progress measures survey. Local partnerships are asked to report the number of high school students participating in job shadowing, mentoring, internships, and apprenticeships. Preliminary indications from aggregate data suggest that most local partnerships need to intensify their efforts to identify all types of work-based learning opportunities.

Integration of Career Information and Guidance

Counselling, career guidance, and related support services are critical elements of effective STW transition programs, not frivolous appendages that can be sacrificed easily when budgets are tight.

Career guidance and counselling are now being built into the STW systems launched with venture capital available under the STWOA. The Act identifies counselling, case management, and linkages with other community services as examples of connecting activities, the third leg of the STW triangle. At the state level, involvement in career guidance and counselling is likely to take such forms as collection and dissemination of labour market information, design and delivery of professional development programs, and training for work site mentors. Local partnerships, which must ultimately bear responsibility for the effective melding of work-based learning and school-based learning, are already collecting information about the number of schools that offer career guidance activities and the number of students who participate in them. Although preliminary progress measures data indicate that a significant percentage of schools are

---

[6]. Ibid., Title I, sec. 103.

offering some type of career awareness or career exploration, there appears to be a need to connect discrete activities into comprehensive career guidance frameworks.

A Sequential, Progressive System that Starts Before Grade 11

Although many people think of STW programs as options for high school juniors and seniors, the most effective initiatives offer a continuum of developmentally appropriate activities for elementary, middle, and high school students. The STWOA's emphasis on serving all students clearly encompasses all grade levels. State system builders and local partnerships are required to offer career awareness, career exploration, and career guidance to students at the earliest possible age (but not later than the seventh grade). Statutory recognition is also given to the importance of including elementary and middle schools in local STW partnerships "as an investment in future workforce productivity and competitiveness".[7] Even though the formal application of STW strategies at the elementary and middle school levels is a fairly recent phenomenon in many communities, more than 530 local partnerships already report that at least 80 percent of their elementary and middle schools offer some type of STW activities (Medrich, Giambattista and Moskovitz 1996). More research will be needed to determine whether these activities are actually influencing curriculum and pedagogy and helping younger students draw initial connections between their current classroom learning and real-life settings.

Post-secondary Options

In order to attract *all* students, STW programs must ensure access to multiple post-secondary options, including two-year and four-year colleges, traditional apprenticeship programs, and other structured education and training options. An initial job or enrolment in some form of post-secondary education or training is not seen as an endpoint, but simply another step in a lifetime of learning. The STWOA explicitly calls for post-secondary participation in local partnerships and state-level STW governance structures, but active engagement of baccalaureate institutions remains a challenge. Almost 70 percent of the 569 local partnerships that completed the post-secondary participation grid on the most recent progress measures survey cited the participation of at least one four-year college, but only 32 percent reported the participation of two or more baccalaureate institutions (Medrich, Giambattista and Moskovitz, 1996). While a growing body of evidence indicates that the pedagogical underpinnings of STW are applicable to all learning, many parents, teachers, counselors, and college admissions personnel remain skeptical of STW as a way to prepare for college. A basic tenet of STW is learner-centered teaching that requires students to think, develop in-depth understanding, and apply what they have learned to important, realistic projects. Nonetheless, most college admissions standards are still based on the Carnegie units developed in the early 1900s as the requisite evidence of academic readiness. Even

---

7. Ibid., sec. 3(a)(6).

though more than 90 percent of U.S. baccalaureate institutions now offer remedial courses and between 40-70 percent of entering freshmen are enrolled in at least one of these courses (Gray 1997), colleges and universities have been slow to adopt admission procedures that allow students to demonstrate knowledge and skills in a variety of ways.

Creative Financing

High-quality STW programs cannot be launched or survive without creative financing strategies. A crucial skill for programme administrators is leveraging, patching together and coordinating funds from a variety of sources. Creative financing lies at the heart of the STWOA. State and local partnerships are required to identify how other resources (including other federal grants) will be coordinated with their emerging STW systems. The Act makes it possible to combine certain types of federal funds and to obtain regulatory and statutory waivers from the U.S. Departments of Education and Labor. Since the grants available under the STWOA are time-limited venture capital rather than annual budget allocations, states and local partnerships are developing their STW efforts with the foreknowledge that they will need to generate other resources or reallocate existing monies to replace the federal funds that flow on a diminishing scale. To help track state and local STW investments, the progress measures survey will ask local partnerships to report the amount of funds received from other public and private sources as well as the value and types of in-kind contributions they have generated.

THE STATE EXPERIENCE WITH STW

Given the U.S. commitment to local control, state experiences with STW implementation are predictably diverse. A 50-state summary of STW initiatives, prepared by the Education Commission of the States (ECS) in 1996 and updated in 1997 (DeLuca 1996), describes the various ways in which states are applying the elements highlighted in the AED study. The ECS summaries demonstrate that all states are moving forward to address the three broad components of the STWOA, but each has different foci-reflecting differences in priorities, historical circumstances, and institutional structures. The three examples that follow illustrate some of the innovative strategies used to implement the STWOA at the state level.

1. New York: Curricular Restructuring

Even though a single Board of Regents governs elementary through post-secondary education in New York, the state had created a mosaic of initiatives in education reform by the late 1980s. *A New Compact for Learning*, issued by the Board in 1991, presented a unified vision of education reform and called for a cooperative, community-based effort to prepare all students for employment and effective citizenship. Seven curricular frameworks were subsequently designed, including one on Career Development and Occupational Studies (CDOS) which was envisioned as a delivery system of applied learning for the other six. CDOS calls for career majors for all students and encourages greater use of authentic assessment. In 1996, the Board began requiring all students to take the challenging Regents Exam for high school graduation.

2. *Colorado: Building Partnerships and Integrating Institutions*

Like New York, Colorado was experiencing myriad state and local education reform efforts by the turn of the decade. The state's response was to concentrate on institutional collaboration. The Colorado legislature mandated competency-based college admissions standards for higher education, necessitating collaboration between post-secondary institutions and the K-12 system. Effective with the class of 1996, graduates of self-selected high schools were able to enter participating post-secondary institutions on the basis of their own school's assessment of their proficiency levels in English, science, mathematics, geography, and history. At present, Colorado is addressing the challenge of assessing the academic content of students' work-based learning experiences.

3. *Wisconsin: Youth Apprenticeships and the Challenge of Scaling Up*

Starting in 1987, Wisconsin school districts were required to provide k-12 students with access to an education-for-employment programme. A 1991 statute created a youth apprenticeship programme that now offers apprenticeship options in 14 programme areas. While these apprenticeship programs have demonstrated positive results, the state is facing limitations on the number of students that can be accommodated in them. Other challenges include forging connections between the apprenticeship programs and post-secondary institutions and between the state's new academic standards and workforce competencies.

WHAT WE EVALUATE IS WHAT WE VALUE: LOOKING BEYOND THE NUMBERS

The experiences of these three states show that efforts to implement STW on a wide scale are laden with challenges. As educators, employers, parents, and other stakeholders come together to create STW systems, they affirm the value of new and innovative connections between learning and work-and build new pathways between educational institutions and the labour market. They are attempting to introduce a new set of values and mores into institutions that have been, historically, intractable in the face of reform efforts.

Is the nation's current interest in STW activities a step toward educating *all* students for meaningful and challenging employment or just the *reform du jour*? As evaluations of STW activities unfold, it will be important for researchers, policy makers, programme operators, and other stakeholders to remain focused on programme improvement. Information about what is and is not working needs to be disseminated in a timely fashion to facilitate mid-course corrections. Mistakes and problems are to be expected in any new system. It is critically important to identify these problems and devise ways to prevent them or respond to them in the future. To determine whether the STW system builders are succeeding, one should look first at the statistics and circumstances that are driving change.

Despite widespread belief that a linear progression from high school to college (and then possibly on to graduate school) is the best route to high paying positions with job security, the vast majority of young Americans do not follow such a pathway. While 70 percent of high school graduates go on to college (Bailey and Merritt 1997), less than 35 percent actually earn a baccalaureate degree, and it takes most of them more than five years to do so (National Centre for Education Statistics 1996). Those who attempt to move directly from high school into the work force find it even more difficult to land high-skill, high-wage jobs. The typical high school graduate bounces from one low-skill or low-wage job to another for almost ten years before finally settling on to a career track.

If STW is making a difference, these numbers should be changing. More and more young Americans should be moving into positions that require high levels of skills and knowledge. Regardless of when they choose to enter the work force, their movement into jobs should reflect years of planning and preparation rather than a series of haphazard choices.

Short-term indicators of process and participation can be used to show movement toward the kind of system envisioned by the STWOA. Possible process indicators include changes in curriculum, pedagogy, assessment, and scheduling. In terms of participation, the system should show steady growth in the number of students, schools, and employers involved in STW activities, as well as changes in the quality (i.e., depth and breadth) of their involvement.

However, the only way to determine whether old patterns are changing and young people are making use of new pathways is to track a sizeable number of STW participants for at least a decade (White 1997). This process needs to start now, with an understanding that STW advocates cannot afford to wait ten years for evidence of success.

A new kind of system requires a new kind of evaluation. As STW systems mature and take root, programme evaluation strategies must become more individualised to document student progress and achievement. When researchers monitor the whereabouts of a STW cohort at regular intervals, they need to look behind the numbers. They need to explore the underlying sequence of choices and thought patterns that led young adults to the positions in which the researchers find them. Is a string of jobs evidence of drifting aimlessly in the labour market or evidence of thoughtful, career-related decisions? Evaluations of STW systems also need to be tailored to the needs and expectations of multiple stakeholders. While improved student achievement and easier transitions from school to the workplace are arguably the most important goals of STW systems, each participating stakeholder comes to the table with a range of questions to be answered. Employers, for example, will want to know how STW activities are affecting their recruitment, hiring, and training processes, and ultimately their bottom lines.

On what basis will the ultimate success of the STW movement be judged? The answer to that question will, of course, depend on whom you ask. However, measurement of the success of STW and its institutionalization as a reform strategy may ultimately be distilled from two key indicators. If large majorities of parents and post-secondary institutions accept STW activities as viable strategies for their children and their students, it will be clear the United States is making fundamental changes in the preparation of young people for productive adult lives.

The opinions in this paper do not necessarily reflect the position or policy of the Academy for Educational Development or the Education Commission of the States, and no official endorsement is implied.

REFERENCES

Bailey, T. and Merritt, D. (1997), *School-to-Work for the College-Bound*, Berkeley, CA: National Center for Research in Vocational Education.

Barton, P. (1991), "The School to Work Transition", *Issues in Science and Technology*, vol. VII, no. 3, pp. 50-51.

Chance, W. (1985), *"...the best of educations"*, The John D. and Catherine T. MacArthur Foundation.

Charner, I. (1996), "School-to-Work Opportunities: Prospects and Challenges," in Kathryn M. Borman et al. (eds.), *Implementing Educational Reform: Sociological Perspectives on Educational Policy"*, Norwood, NJ: Ablex, pp. 146-155.

Charner, I. et al. (1995), "Reforms of the School-to-Work Transition: Findings, Implications, and Challenges," *Phi Delta Kappan,* September.

Corbett, H. D. and Wilson, B. (1990), *Testing, Reform, and Rebellion*, Norwood, NY: Ablex, 1990.

Cuban, L. (1995), *Tinkering Toward Utopia*, Cambridge, MA: Harvard University Press, p. 81.

DeLuca, D. (1996), *Profiles in Connecting Learning and Work: State Initiatives*, Denver: Education Commission of the States.

de Tocqueville, A. (1945), *Democracy in America*, trans. Henry Reeve, rev. ed. Phillips Bradley, New York: Vintage, vol. I, p.318.

Medrich, E., Giambattista, J. and Moskovitz, R. (1996), *School-to-Work Progress Measures Report: January 1 - June 30 1996,* Berkeley, CA: MPR Associate.

Gray, K. (1996), "The Baccalaureate Game: Is It Right for All Teens?" *Phi Delta Kappan,* April, cited in Bailey and Merritt (1997), *School-to-Work for the College-Bound*, Berkeley, CA: National Center for Research in Vocational Education, p. 7.

Gray, K. (1997), "The Baccalaureate Game," cited in Bailey, T. and Merritt, D. (1997), *School-to-Work for the College-Bound*, Berkeley, CA: National Center for Research in Vocational Education, p. 8.

Kosmahl Aring, M. (1993), "What the `V' Word is Costing America's Economy," *Phi Delta Kappan*, January 1993; cited in Mendel, R. (1994), "The American School-to-Career Movement: A Background Paper for Policy Makers and Foundation Officers", Washington D.C.: American Youth Policy Forum, p. 2.

Kyle, R. (1995), *School-to-Work Transition and Its Role in the Systemic Reform of Education: The Experience of Jefferson County Kentucky and the Kentucky Education Reform Act*, Washington, D.C.: National Institution for Work and Learning, Academy for Educational Development.

Matthews, A. (1997), *Bright College Years*, New York: Simon & Schuster.

Mendel, R. (1994), "The American School-to-Career Movement: A Background Paper for Policy Makers and Foundation Officers", Washington D.C.: American Youth Policy Forum, p. 2.

National Center for Education Statistics (1996), *The Condition of Education*, Washington, D.C.: U.S. Department of Education, p. 93.

National Commission on Excellence in Education (1983), *A Nation at Risk*, Washington, D.C.: U.S. Department of Education, p. 1.

National Education Goals Panel (1996), *The National Education Goals Panel Report 1996: A Nation of Learners*, Washington, D.C., p. xv.

Rumpf, E. L. (1997), "Vocational Education in the Schools: Secondary Schools," *Encyclopedia of Education*, vol. 10, p. 499.

Sarason, S. (1990), *The Predictable Failure of School Reform*, San Francisco: Jossey-Bass, Inc., p. 13.

The Secretary's Commission on Achieving Necessary Skills (1992), *Learning a Living: A Blueprint for High Performance*, Washington, D.C.: U.S. Department of Labor, p. 6.

White, R. (1997), "Evaluating Students' Work-based Learning Opportunities, *State Education Leader,* vol. 14, no. 2., p. 8.

Wise, A. (1979), *Legislated Learning*, Berkeley, CA: The University of California Press; cited in Michael Fullan (1991), *The New Meaning of Educational Change*, New York: Teachers College Press, p. 18.

CHAPTER 3

FIRM BASED VOCATIONAL EDUCATION IN SWEDEN - A NEW SUCCESSFUL CONCEPT?*·

ANDERS NILSSON

INTRODUCTION

The difficulties for young people to find employment are usually explained by a malfunctioning labour market, including rigidities and insider-outsider phenomena, or by mismatch problems caused by rapidly changing demand patterns to which the entrants in the labour market have not adjusted. For several reasons, policy makers have concentrated on the mismatch problem by launching a large number of competence and skills programmes. During the last decade, programmes aimed at an increasing volume of high-quality vocational education have been much in vogue in practically all industrialised countries, with the USA as a notable exception and the Japanese on-the-job training system as a special case (Shackleton et al. 1995). This is particularly true in the European Union, where several such programmes have been launched to enhance the volume and quality in vocational training.

Sweden is one of the countries where vocational training has been strongly promoted. One interesting feature of the Swedish policy is that new organisational forms of training have emerged. From the 1940's onwards, a large part of the vocational education has been carried out by public authorities, and since the early 1970's, this is the case for almost all vocational education. Up to the late 1980's, the central government was either directly or indirectly responsible. Recently, however, responsibility and the fiscal means have been shifted to the municipalities. This

* This chapter presents preliminary results of the research project "The Building-up of Competence and the Use of Knowledge - Vocational and Upper Secondary Education in the Transformation of Society", financed by the Swedish Board of Education, grant no 15002. I am grateful to Christer Lundh and Lars Pettersson for comments and, above all, to all the interviewees who have put their time and expertise at my disposal.

decentralisation also implies that the previously uniform system has become somewhat more diversified. Furthermore, the possibilities for firms to participate in vocational education have increased. Some firms, in particular in the manufacturing industry, have seized upon this opportunity and invested quite substantially in various forms of vocational education. The purpose of this chapter is to present and discuss these forms of vocational education, why they started, how they are run, and what to expect of them. In particular, the chapter presents an industry-specific analysis by concentrating on vocational education in the manufacturing sector.

THEORETICAL POINT OF DEPARTURE

This chapter is based on public choice theory (Olson 1984). However, the theory's utilisation in this paper is rather crude. It implies that a government (at the national or at the local level) designs its institutions as a result of the outcome of a struggle between different power groups. Such a struggle could be expected to be particularly intense, and easy to identify, in periods when basic conditions have been altered. Such was the case during the 1940's and early 1950's, when a "Swedish model" was established in the field of vocational education. At a turbulent time around 1990, the "model" was changed drastically as responsibility was transferred from the national level to the municipalities. What followed was a transformation of the explicit and uniform Swedish model of vocational education into several implicit models at the local level. These new forms emerged partly as a reaction to the failure of the existing system to provide labour with necessary skills.

To this day there has been wide-spread dissatisfaction among firms with the quality of the vocational programmes offered by the municipalities. The inability of the authorities "to deliver" is probably an important explanation of the present development. Different groups, more or less well organised, try to change the contents as well as the organisational forms of vocational education to suit their own particular interests. Examples of such groups include politicians and administrators with a particular interest in education, teachers, trade unions, and local firms. The hypothesis of this paper is that firms constitute the single most important interest group and that, consequently, the varying organisational forms of different municipalities reflect the local firms' relative strength.

A number of reasons lie behind the decision to single out, hypothetically, firms as the most important interest group. The basic reason is the changing character of labour demand. The industrial structure has moved away from standardised production and new demands for skills and competencies have emerged (Rees 1994). These include a better general knowledge of, above all, mathematics and written communication, but, as a recent Swedish study underlines, also the ability to plan and carry out work without direct supervision (Axelsson 1996). These changes in labour demand are derived from new technical systems and new organisational models in firms.

The relative strength of firms is not easy to operationalise. Here, the assertion is made that, in the case where one firm is dominant in a municipality, this firm has a great potential strength, whereas potential strength is assumed to be weaker in municipalities with a more diversified economic structure. However, this potential may not be realised. To name but one complication, municipalities with one dominant firm often tend to have a strong local trade union as a counterpart.

The analysis is based on interviews with representatives of groups that are (or could expected to be) actors in the area of "vocational education", in the southern Swedish region of Skåne. In particular, they have been asked how vocational education in the manufacturing industry is organised in their municipality and how firms contribute to this educational process. Furthermore, some specific questions have been asked to map out the motives for various groups to engage in (or be indifferent to) vocational education. Finally, the representatives of our interest groups have been asked what they expect from a system of vocational education. Representatives from most of the potential interest groups have been interviewed. They include the divisional heads of the regional bureau of The Swedish National Board of Education; personnel responsible for vocational education at the municipality level and/or at the school level (i.e. administrators, school principals, etc.); representatives of firm-based vocational schools; representatives of local firms; and one trade union representative. All in all, the paper is based on a total of 30 interviews, carried out between October 1996 and March 1997.[3]

FOUR MODELS OF VOCATIONAL EDUCATION

For a long time, vocational education aimed at the manufacturing industry was organised in a uniform, school-based manner throughout the country. In the 1970s and during most of the 1980s, it was organised on the basis of "workshop techniques," (*verkstadsteknisk linje*)[4] - a two-year programme where emphasis was laid on the acquisition of practical skills. The programme provided training that was useful in the prevailing industrial organisation of the 1970s. During the 1980s, this situation changed. Technical and organisational change in manufacturing industry implied that existing programmes to an increasing extent were regarded as being obsolete (Nilsson 1994). As a result, vocational education was re-organised into three-year programmes with a larger theoretical component than was previously the case. One of these, the industrial programme (*industriprogrammet*), is the successor of "workshop techniques". Although still a rather uniform programme it includes possibilities for adaptation to local conditions. However, dissatisfaction with the programme has risen as the number of students who failed or barely passed their theoretical education has increased.

---

[3] Details are available from the author upon request.

[4] There exists no official translation of several key concepts in the Swedish vocational education system. Where this is the case, the approximate English term is put in quotation marks and, in addition, the Swedish term is given when the term appears for the first time in the paper.

In response, some alternative models of vocational education have emerged during the past few years. The new programmes have come into existence so recently that no students have as yet finished their vocational education. However, some of the effects on recruitment patterns are already known. At present, four different models of vocational education in the manufacturing sector can be discerned in the region.

The industrial programme

The industrial programme is a three-year, full time secondary education and one of the sixteen national programmes in existence. About one-fourth of the time spent is devoted to theoretical subjects, slightly more than 50 percent consists of vocational subjects, and in the remaining 20% the student can choose between other largely vocational modules. A characteristic feature of the programme is based on "education in workshops" (*arbetsförlagd utbildning*), which implies that at least 15 weeks should be spent on company-based lessons. This poses new demands on firms, and a large number of them decline to take part in the new system. Thus a paradoxical situation has arisen. Although the industrial programme allows for more time at, and a closer collaboration with, practice-oriented workshops, the situation is in places worse now than it was with the two-year programme.

This is one major problem in the industrial programme. Another is the fact that the programme enjoys a very low status among students. Few students apply for entry to the programme, and those that do tend to have low motivation and very low grades from the comprehensive school. They are, in other words, "low quality students". The low quality characteristic of the programme reinforces the firms' reluctance to provide the students with "education in workshops". Many representatives of the firms a) do not believe that the students are able to profit from "education in workshops" and b) do not intend to hire them after school, anyway.

As a result of these difficulties several alternatives have emerged. One of the alternatives considered is a renewal of the old apprenticeship system.

The apprenticeship system

In Sweden, the apprenticeship system had a strong standing well into the 1950's, but it became subsequently regarded as an outdated system. With the establishment of an integrated secondary school system in 1971, including vocational education, apprenticeships became a rare exception.[5] Still, our interviews have made it evident that in many firms the absence of an apprenticeship system has been regretted. The decentralisation of upper secondary education has initiated a discussion to re-institute apprenticeship systems. However, although it seems fair to characterise industrial education in a few municipalities as "pseudo-apprenticeship," a full scale system has materialised in only one place in the region. In the municipality of Svedala,

---

[5] A not very precise but the best available measure of apprenticeship education is provided by the number of applications for government subsidies for this type of education. The number decreased from about 2,500 in 1969 to about 1,000 during the 1970's (excluding applications in the building industry).

apprenticeships have been made available to a limited number of students from the autumn term in 1996.

The main motive to engage in an apprenticeship system is to secure a long term, high quality labour supply. The apprenticeship programme of Svedala is more demanding than an ordinary upper secondary programme. The students study theoretical subjects to the same extent that students of the industrial programme do, but in addition spend the remainder of a normal working week in job-related training. The students have to be highly motivated and, generally, quite able. The problem for the firm lies in the recruitment of such students. Firms try to overcome these difficulties by providing a range of explicit and implicit benefits. In addition to an apprentice wage-system students are (implicitly) guaranteed employment after a successful completion of the programme. Furthermore, promising students are given opportunities to earn some extra money by working during weekends. They are also first in line for the much sought after summer jobs.

These incentives have been successful. The apprenticeship programme is much more attractive to prospective students than the traditional industrial programme. Notwithstanding this attraction, however, in most municipalities where the possibility to initiate an apprentice programme has been considered, it has been rejected. The main reason for this seems to be doubts as to whether the benefits will outweigh the costs. In many firms, no new labour is being hired, which naturally implies that recruitment benefits do not apply. Other firms are committed to future recruitment but are still hesitant to meet the respective costs, especially since successful students would be attractive and much sought-after in the labour market, and thus expensive to keep.

Firm-based schooling

The apprenticeship system is one model for firms taking the full responsibility for vocational education. The other is a firm's own secondary school, i. e. an educational institution run entirely by a company. In principle, there is little difference between an apprenticeship system and a firm-based school. They are both initiated and run by a firm, with the explicit purpose to furnish that firm with its specific need of competence. The difference in theoretical instruction between the two is mainly a consequence of different competence needs. However, the practical consequences of running a school rather than an apprenticeship system are substantial. An apprenticeship is a form of employment, which implies that the firms' rules for admission, possible dismissal, regulations for day-releases, etc. take precedence over school regulations. A firm-based school, however, must adhere to the same regulations that municipal schools do. Not unlike apprenticeships, firm-based schools have been widely discussed, but at present only one school has been established in the region.

Firm-based schools are, throughout Sweden, only run by large export-oriented companies such as Volvo, Scania or ABB. It is also these companies which question the quality of today's Swedish vocational school system. The regional example of a firm-based school is that of Perstorp AB - a modern, process-oriented firm with a world-wide organisation for the production and sale of chemical products. The reason for starting a school of its own was to secure a long-term supply of qualified labour rather than to having to rely on narrowly educated personnel trained by traditional forms of vocational schooling.

Perstorp has put some substantial resources into firm-based schooling. This includes well-equipped school premises that are being let to the school on very favourable terms. The firm also defrays all costs of an annual practice period in one of the firm's subsidiaries abroad, and all indirect costs for supervision when the students practice at the firm-level. Other running costs, however, are met by the municipalities. The school is recognised by the school authorities and, consequently, each municipality is obliged to cover the cost for each student admitted to the programme. It is interesting to note that no explicit benefits, such as a guaranteed employment, are offered. Representatives of the firm-based school argue that the education must be of such a high standard that prospective students apply for it because of its quality, not because of any additional benefits. This concept has proved to be extremely successful. A large number of students have applied to the programme and only those with top marks from the comprehensive school have been admitted. This implies that a large percentage proportion of them is likely to continue their studies at university level after secondary schooling has come to en end. Although this could be seen as a potential threat to the firm's recruitment targets, Perstorp AB is confident that the students will become impregnated with "company culture" during their studies and will return to the company after their university studies.

The technical programme

The fourth model is similar to firm-based schooling in that it combines extensive theoretical studies with vocational education, and it includes a substantial involvement by firms. However, it is an integral part of the municipal system. Technical programmes have been introduced, above all, in medium sized towns with long lasting industrial traditions and with an established upper secondary school. The actual structure of the programme differs between the towns, but the core consists of theoretical studies of social or natural sciences. The contents of the practical component differ according to the needs of the co-operating firms. In Trelleborg, for instance, continuous processing techniques are important, whereas in Eslöv mechanics and engineering are much more prominent.

The technical programme meets several demands from both firms and municipalities. It is built around a group of firms (not one firm as in the case of firm-based schooling) which implies an element of cost-sharing among the firms. It also implies - from a firm's point of view - that each firm's possibility to observe and assess prospective workers during the training periods is somewhat limited since several firms are involved. The assessment possibilities are still considerable, however, since the students spend most of their firm-based education in two or three firms.

The most important reason to start a technical programme, both from the municipality's and from the firms' point of view, is to improve the recruitment to industrial training programmes. In the information given to students, it is emphasised that the new programme is characterised by high quality instruction, and that the students have access to modern equipment. It has also been deemed advantageous to give the programme a new name (technical programme or T 2000) in order to distance itself from the low status the traditional industrial programme enjoys. As a further means of persuasion, tangible incentives are applied. In most cases, students of the technical programme are first in line for summer jobs and, in addition, guaranteed at least one year of employment after successful studies.

The recruitment effects have been impressive in the two municipalities where the co-operation model has been in operation for a year. In the traditional industrial programme it has often been difficult to recruit a sufficient number of applicants. In the technical programmes, around one out of three applicants have been accepted, implying an increase in the quality of the students. The school administrators responding to our survey did not foresee any difficulties for these students to pursue their theoretical studies in a successful manner, nor have there been any reported drop-outs when the practical modules of the programmes have commenced.

A STRUGGLE FOR INFLUENCE OVER VOCATIONAL EDUCATION?

In the introduction, a hypothesis was formulated where vocational education is seen as an arena where several interest group struggle to exert their influence over the contents of education and training. In particular, it was assumed that firms would try to increase their influence at the expense of the municipalities.

A closer look at trade unions and local politicians will provide some first indications as to whether our hypothesis is universally applicable. There is little evidence from our interviews that trade union representatives have been important in the re-modelling of vocational education. This does not imply that they have been entirely passive; in some municipalities trade union representatives take a vivid interest in the organisation of education and training. There are, however, no indications that local trade unions pursue a particular policy. The evidence rather points to a collaboration between firms and local trade unions; indeed, school authorities often refer to them jointly as "the industry." With the possible exception of a couple of municipalities where the traditional industrial programme prevails, the trade unions are unquestionably the junior partner in that collaboration. As for local politicians, the representatives of school authorities and of firms have been asked explicit questions about the role of politicians. Invariably, all respondents have claimed that vocational education is not an issue in local politics. Furthermore, in most municipalities the politicians are seen as being dispassionate in these matters. Individual exceptions exist, but when the new forms of vocational education have been discussed, it emerged that municipal politicians have played no important roles. These are no final verdicts, since the assessment of the trade unions and local politicians rely mainly on other parties' evidence. Provisionally, however, it seems safe to conclude that any potential struggle about the main influences over vocational education focuses on firms and school authorities. In what follows we will examine the evidence from each party and use the school authorities' points of view as a point for departure.

Opinions of school authorities on firms' increasing participation in vocational education

The necessity of firms' participation in vocational education has always been recognised by school authorities, even if the desirability of such co-operation was sometimes questioned during the 1970's. However, the introduction of three-year programmes has put increased demands on the quality of firms' participation. Whereas firms previously provided students with some work experience, they are now required to provide "education in workshops". Firms must furnish the students with not only supervision but also some education. Small firms in particular have found this too demanding and decline to participate in vocational education.

The relative reluctance of firms to participate in vocational education is a reality which schools have learnt to handle. The new, and opposite, situation where firms are not only willing to participate but also put demands on school activities, however, seems to be more difficult to cope with. This is in particular the case in the region where firm-based schooling has been established. It has succeeded in recruiting high-quality students, not only in their own, but also in the surrounding municipalities. This nominally vocational programme is actually competing for students who would otherwise choose theoretical programmes in upper secondary schools in the surrounding municipalities. The school authorities in these municipalities are compelled by law to cover the average national cost for students who participate in these industrial programmes. It thus comes as no surprise that the attitude of school authorities in the surrounding municipalities towards firm-based schooling is ambiguous.

There is, on the one hand, some pride and satisfaction that the region is able to offer an education of extremely high quality. On the other hand, the difference in resources between firm-based schooling and the municipal schools is so considerable that the equality between the two types of schooling is questioned. However, in practice these doubts have been largely overcome. Firm-based educational institutions "buy" practically all theoretical instructions from upper secondary schools in the surrounding municipalities. In that sense, a certain degree of symbiosis exists. In fact, this has been carried even further in the technical programme where firms take care of the practical arrangements and have some influence on the overall modelling of the programme. If conflicts have emerged in that process, they have not been revealed during our interviews

In sum, the school authorities do not claim that there has been a struggle for influence over vocational education as long as the overall control remains in the hands of the municipality. Companies, however, may perceive these arrangements differently.

Company motives for engaging in vocational education

Two company motives for engaging in vocational education stand out. The first is to secure higher qualifications among the newly employed; the second is to retain the newly employed within their organisations. The latter is not a big problem in large firms located in small communities, i. e. where apprenticeships have long been the favoured system of vocational education. The large firm is the only important industrial employer and working there is associated with a certain status in the community. The trainee is aware of the fact that he has not only been admitted to a vocational education but also to a probable employment by the dominant firm. For the firm, therefore, there is little reason to believe that the trainee will seek employment elsewhere.

The situation is similar with firm-based schooling, with one important exception. The firm is the dominant industrial employer in the municipality and has a good reputation as an employer. However, the firm's school policy to recruit very talented students implies that a large percentage proportion is likely to continue their studies at universities or colleges. Some students might be persuaded to seek employment directly after schooling has come to an end. The majority, however, must be convinced that the firm is also an attractive employer for persons with a university or college degree. To a limited extent, *firm-specific training* becomes an investment in human capital which the students may find difficult to exploit elsewhere and, consequently, may be an inducement to seek employment with the firm after university studies have been completed. More important, however, is the possibility (and challenge) to familiarise students with a *firm specific culture* during their studies at the upper secondary level.

The possibility to retain well-educated students in their organisations is an equally important motive for firms to engage in the "technical programme". However, this model which is less costly and requires less engagement than firm-based schooling, makes it more difficult for each firm to fulfil specific staff aspirations. Several firms are involved in each programme and the opportunities to provide students with firm-specific human capital and a firm-specific culture are limited. Benefits, such as job guarantees or subsidised practice periods abroad, are means through which the participating firms hope to counteract the potentially greater mobility among students in these programmes.

Finally, it is important to explain why Swedish firms are eager to secure recruitment. The manufacturing industry has shrunk considerably during the last 5-6 years and the prospects of any considerable increase in the number of employees in the years ahead are far from being promising. However, there are also some strong demographic effects which need to be taken into account. In Sweden, the remainder of the 1990s and the early new millennium will be characterised by a diminishing number of people aged 16-20. In other words the recruitment base is shrinking. In addition, a substantial increase in the number of retirements is expected to take place over the next two decades. Thus, the efforts of firms should only partially be seen in the light of problems to recruit competent personnel today. There is also a long-term strategy involved, where in particular large companies do not believe that their long term recruitment requirements can be adequately met by the public educational system.

This suggestion is borne out by representatives of firm-based schooling. Here, the motive is not only to increase recruitment to the company, but also to demonstrate that firms can and should take a bigger responsibility for the overall vocational education in society. As one of the survey's respondents put it:

"We don't want to just join in with the complaints about an inadequate modern vocational education, we want to offer a private alternative which is at least as good as the best which the municipal system can provide."

Thus, the companies' motives are quite complex and range from attempts to change to overall educational policy to securing an effective labour supply. Over the last decade firms have increased their influence over vocational education, even though school authorities have not admitted any retreat.

CONCLUDING REMARKS

The relative failure of the municipalities to provide firms with their desired competences has undoubtedly been the most important factor when it comes to explaining why local models of vocational education have emerged. Various organisational forms are used where quality levels differ markedly. This is a striking contrast to the previous uniform system of Swedish vocational education.

The hypothesis formulated in the introduction implied that firms' interests in influencing vocational education has been the single most important factor in explaining the precise organisation in different municipalities. Although the hypothesis has not been subjected to any rigorous tests, our interviews have not presented any evidence of actual "power struggles" between firms, schools, and trade unions. However, there exists an overall pattern of adaptation to rapidly changing economic conditions. These changes make it difficult for municipal schools to keep up with the technological pace (machinery, soft-ware. etc.) . Only competitive firms possess the human and fiscal capability to be at the technological frontier. This then means that if schools want firms as partners in vocational education, they have to be open to different local forms of co-operation. This dependency has transferred power over vocational education to firms. Thus, in a strict sense our hypothesis has neither been refuted nor confirmed. Power has been transferred, but not as a result of serious conflicts.

The hypothesis further predicted that such a transfer would be more extensive in municipalities where one big firm had a strong position in the local economy. This part of the hypothesis is supported by our evidence, although far from conclusively since no attempt has been made to establish the firms' relative strength. It is telling, however, that Perstorp, where firm-based schooling is located, and Svedala, with an apprenticeship system in place, are both municipalities dominated by the firm that runs these educational institutions. On the other hand, the industrial programme where firms do not possess much influence over vocational education, is at work in all the four larger cities in the region. Here, the economic structure is more varied and no single firm is dominant in the manufacturing industry. In addition, the industrial programme is at work in a couple of municipalities, dominated by very small firms (Osby, Hässleholm, and Ängelholm). Judging from such an approximate measurement of firms' relative strength in the different municipalities, our hypothesis is corroborated.

The interpretation of the results can be carried a little further. The rapid technological and organisational changes have altered demand patterns in the labour market to the extent that modern firms require competences which the traditional industrial vocational programmes seldom provide. Thus, although there is little or no evidence of "power struggles," the overall outcome of these changes is that firms now possess a lot more influence over vocational education than previously. Our result that actual "power struggles" have not taken place indicates that firms' relative strength has been exerted in more subtle ways. It seems as if the actual organisational structure of the different programmes reflects, to a very large extent, local demand patterns in terms of industrial competences. The traditional industrial programme and, to a somewhat lesser extent the apprenticeship system, provide their students and trainees with forms of competences that are valid only in parts of the manufacturing sector. Both systems provide some up-grading of theoretical knowledge. The recruitment pattern to these programmes, however, has been left largely unaltered: young males with low to medium grades from comprehensive schools but in possession of certain, often considerable, practical skills dominate the intake. The fact that large international companies have engaged in apprenticeship programmes implies that such traditional competences are still in demand, even in production processes aimed at the world market. However, the emphasis put on selection criteria by the firm responsible for the existing apprenticeship programme also implies that formal competences are necessary, but not sufficient conditions for success. Personal characteristics are of extreme importance (Johansson 1997), and the industrial programme has never been efficient in such selection processes.

The different recruitment strategies of students to firm-based schooling (including the technical programme), on the other hand, signify a new tendency. Here, emphasis is less on practical skills and more on a theoretical understanding of the processes that underlie industrial production.

The emergence of several models of vocational education is, from a strictly economic standpoint, a promising development. It demonstrates that the degree of flexibility in the educational system increases and that students have a real choice between different forms of vocational education. It also, however, raises fears of an increasingly dual vocational education system. The different recruitment patterns point in that direction but they also reflect that the segmentation of the labour market in the manufacturing industry is changing its character. The previous, and in many places still existing, differentiation between blue- and white-collar workers *within* the firm seems to be replaced by a differentiation *between* firms. In firms with "flat organisations" and "continuous flows" all workers must be able to master administrative as well as operational tasks. Firm-based schooling, and to some extent even the apprenticeship system, prepare the students very well for this type of work. It is doubtful, however, whether the traditional industrial programme lives up to these expectations.

Our discussion indicates that the tendencies of firms to exercise their influence over vocational education will continue. The current trends in labour market demand and in economic structural change point in that direction. To the extent that this possibility is realised, it is likely to contribute to increasing quality in vocational education. However, it also raises the question of inequality in access to vocational education. The difference in resources between programmes is likely to increase in a system of firm-based vocational education, since the possibility and propensity to supply resources differs markedly between firms. Increasing quality differences in a more diversified system are perhaps unavoidable and a necessary price to pay. But, as the experience of the apprenticeship programme demonstrates, firms are prone to use not only grades from the comprehensive school as selection criteria. Increasing quality differences will certainly imply increasing selectivity. A not too distant future can be envisaged, where promising students with desirable personal characteristics will enjoy an education and a training environment with ample resources and of a high quality. However, there is a distinct risk that the less fortunate students will be directed to municipal programmes of a low quality and only few resources.

In the long run, these changes may lead to a situation where traditional industrial programmes will be abandoned altogether - a scenario not without difficulties. At present, the industrial programme is active mainly in larger cities where the economic structure complicates the development towards a truly firm-based vocational education. There is no single firm big enough to handle all the firm-based activities, and the number of small and medium-sized firms is so large that co-ordination problems will inevitably arise if firms were to take some joint responsibility for the delivery of vocational education. However, the dissatisfaction with the programme and the existence of successful alternatives in neighbouring municipalities will bring about drastic changes, potentially on the lines of apprenticeship-like systems. This is not just a possible regional solution to the problem. A proposal has recently been put forward by the Swedish Minister of Schools which envisages the combination of some of the vocational programmes with some elements of apprenticeships at the national level.

REFERENCES

Axelsson, B. (1996), *Kompetens för konkurrenskraft. Källor, drivkrafter och metoder för kompetensutveckling i företag*, Stockholm, SNS Förlag.

Johansson, S. (1997), "Selection Principles in the Recruitment for Work on the Shop Floor", paper presented at the Swedish-German seminar on recent development in vocational education and training, Umeå september 1997 (mimeo).

Nilsson, A. (1994), "Visions and Labour Demand. The Planning of Vocational Education for the Swedish Manufacturing Industry 1950-1993", *Lund Papers in Economic History*, no 39.

Olofsson, J. (1997), "Arbetsmarknadens yrkesråd. Parterna och yrkesutbildningen 1930-1970", *Lund Papers in Economic History*, no 59.

Olson, M. (1984*), The Rise and Decline of Nations. Economic Growth, Stagflation and Social Rigidities*, London.

Rees, G. (1994), "IT and Vocational Education and Training in Europe: An Overview", in Ducatel, K (ed.), *Employment and Technical Change in Europe. Work Organization, Skills and Training*, Edward Elgar Publishing, Aldershot.

Shackleton, J. R., Clarke, L., Lange, T. and Walsh, S. (1995), *Training for Employment in Western Europe and the United States*, Edward Elgar Publishing, Aldershot.

CHAPTER 4

DIFFERENT SCHOOL SYSTEMS - DIFFERENT LABOUR MARKET RESULTS

STEFAN C. WOLTER, JÖRG CHRISTOFFEL AND MONICA CURTI

INTRODUCTION

As the 20th century draws to a close, unemployment has become the most urgent problem of industrialised economies. Until the oil shock of the mid-1970s, many commentators in the West assumed that the massive unemployment of the 1920s and 1930s was merely a blip on the screen. In the 1970s, however, unemployment rose again, to haunt one industrial nation after another. In virtually all of the countries affected - with the notable exception of the majority of so-called "Anglo-Saxon countries" - unemployment has been characterised by at least two unpalatable features: the first is a failure of response to the upside of the economic cycle, witnessed in the boom years of the mid-1980s. The second is the extent to which young people have been affected by joblessness, in particular the large number of school-leavers who have not been completely integrated in the competitive labour market. These two phenomena are closely linked, and both represent a serious threat for the future.

Until the beginning of the 1990s, Switzerland seemed to have been miraculously spared by the unemployment problems of its neighbours. Even at times when the economy was beginning to flag, both in the 1970s and 1980s, the rates of unemployment in Switzerland never strayed far from the 1 per cent mark. The general rule of full employment applied equally to young Swiss, who managed the transition from school to the world of work without much difficulty (Wolter 1988, p. 14).

Since the recession of 1991, however, and the subsequent stagnation of general economic activity in Switzerland over the last six years, the rate of unemployment has caught up, at nearly 6 per cent is comparable to that of a number of other nations and surpasses the rates of the USA and Japan. This new unemployment has brought with it two associated phenomena, familiar in neighbouring countries of Europe: youth unemployment and long-term unemployment. At present, the latter fluctuates between a quarter and a third of all jobless persons.

The objective of this chapter is to look at the influence of the school system on the success of the labour market, and at the way in which the transition occurs from the former to the latter. The study is based on the hypothesis that different school systems lead to different results in the labour market, in other words that they can either help or hinder the transition of school-leavers to the labour market. The comparison is based on two different Swiss linguistic regions: French and German.

AN INTERNATIONAL COMPARISON OF YOUTH UNEMPLOYMENT

In Diagram 1, a simple graphic and econometric view of youth unemployment across 18 different industrial nations shows clearly that in general terms young people (herein defined as those under 25 years of age) are more affected by unemployment than the numerical average of all other age groups. With just a few exceptions, all of these countries lie to the left of the proportional line, indicating a high degree of youth involvement. It is interesting to note, however, that there are exceptions, which, in a multiple regression, stand out significantly from the remaining countries. The countries in question are Germany (D), Switzerland (CH), and, to a slightly lesser extent, Austria (A). These three countries are distinguished by very different unemployment rates, but have in common the extent to which young people are affected by unemployment. Another similarity is, of course, the long tradition of dual education and training experienced in all three countries, i.e. the combination of practical and theoretical training designed specifically to meet the requirements of the labour market.

A simple multiple regression demonstrates that it is possible to explain about 90 percent of the international difference in youth unemployment ("youth"), with the difference in total unemployment ("total"), a dummy which distinguishes between dual-education countries (Austria, Germany and Switzerland) and others ("dual"), and a variable, which takes the differences between the unemployment rates of young men and women into account ("difmf"), as our explanatory variables.

The regression in Equation 1 (with t-values in parentheses) shows that on average, youth unemployment corresponds to the average national rate of unemployment multiplied by a factor of 1.8. The three dual-education countries experience youth unemployment which is roughly 4.5 percentage points lower than other countries in a comparable situation. The third variable shows that youth unemployment is particularly high in those countries where female rates of unemployment are particularly pronounced. In other words, unemployment seems to be particularly high in those countries where the integration of women in the labour market, for whatever reasons, is difficult.

youth =   0.7 + 1.8 total - 4.5 dual + 0.36 difmf   (1)
            (0.5) (7.70)   (-2.72)   (2.61)
$R^2 = 0.92$, S.E. of regression = 3.35

Diagram 1

Total unemployment and youth unemployment in 18 selected OECD countries in 1995
(Data source: Eurostat and SLFS)

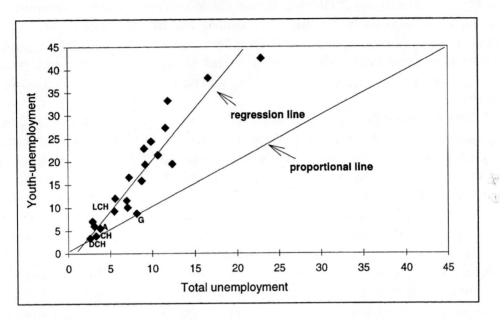

We are thus able to show that in the context of youth unemployment the countries which share the Germanic tradition of a dual education system are significantly different from other nations. Moreover, we are able to support this finding by means of a further differentiation of Switzerland into its main language regions.

If we divide Switzerland into two linguistic regions (see Diagram 1), the German (DCH) and Latin (LCH) areas, and assume that only the German-speaking region operates a Germanic dual education system, then we can integrate these two linguistic regions as separate variables in the regression equation. It then becomes clear that the unemployment rates in both linguistic regions vary between the boundaries of significance given by the equation, i.e. they can be explained by the circumstances assumed in the equation. Since there are no significant differences in the unemployment of young men and women in either region, the differences can be attributed on the one hand to regional variations in unemployment, and on the other to an additional difference, simulated by a dummy variable.

This particular international comparison has the advantage of putting the Swiss data into a wider context. However, the data used are insufficiently differentiated to provide a definitive explanation of the differences, or for us to attempt to assume a relationship of causality. We shall therefore analyse the differences, both those in the educational systems and those in the labour market as a whole, in greater depth.

REGIONAL DIFFERENCES IN THE SCHOOL SYSTEMS OF SWITZERLAND

Switzerland's linguistic and cultural diversity is reflected in its educational systems which show some considerable variations. This diversity can be explained to a great extent by the autonomy which the Swiss cantons, as decentralised centres of government, enjoy in most fields, including that of education. The federal nature of the Swiss educational system leads not only to differences between the two main language regions, the German-speaking and French-speaking areas, but equally to a number of differences within a given language region, especially when we take the degree of urbanisation into account.

Secondary level II (or upper secondary level education) is the first stage of the post-compulsory school education in Switzerland. This includes all of the vocation-oriented and general training options which last at least one year. About 90% of all young Swiss pass through the secondary level II (OECD 1996) - a high rate, even by international standards. By far the most important form of training in this context is on-the-job vocational training, which lasts either three or four years, depending on the trade or profession. In statistical terms, more than three out of four young people in secondary level II are involved in vocational training. On-the-job vocational training is one of the few educational areas which is the responsibility of the federal rather than the cantonal authorities. The second important area at secondary level II is the academic secondary school which leads to university access. Some 22 per cent of all young people in secondary level II go to secondary or "prep" schools that prepare students for higher education. It can already be seen from these few statistics that at secondary level II in Switzerland, vocational training plays a far greater role than general educational schools. There are, however, some considerable differences in attitudes to education at this level between the two linguistic regions. Swiss school statistics show that, whereas in German-speaking Switzerland about one in four young people at secondary level II choose educational options at UEC-level and O-level intermediate schools, the proportion rises to 40 per cent in the Latin language areas.

The educational structures, and to an even greater extent the attitudes to education, differ from one linguistic region to another also at the tertiary level, both in universities and in other higher education institutions. The preference for vocational training, as opposed to a general education at secondary level II, is not without consequences in terms of demand for continuing education at the tertiary level. In 1994, about three times more young adults in Switzerland completed tertiary non-university education (including Higher Business and Administration or Technical Colleges) than graduated from university.

Not unlike tendencies in secondary education, we find that regional differences remain significant.

At termination of post-secondary education, we find that in German-speaking Switzerland the proportion of youngsters graduating from an Higher Technical College amounts to about 30 per cent, whilst the proportion of university graduates amounts to just 6 per cent. The corresponding proportions in French-speaking Switzerland amount to 20 per cent and 9 per cent, respectively. Diagram 2 summarises these statistics. Academic study is thus more prevalent in the French-speaking part of the country than in the German-speaking region - incidentally a mirror image of post-secondary education in France and Germany. However, the proportion of young adults who have benefited from some kind of tertiary-level education is highest in German-speaking Switzerland.

Diagram 2

Swiss students according to language region and type of education
(Data source: [3])

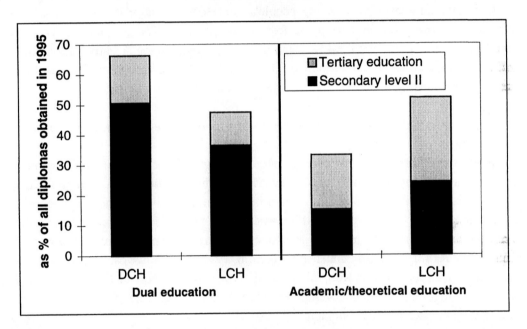

The minimum period of study required at all universities in German-speaking Switzerland is eight semesters (cf. Bundesamt für Statistik 1996). This is also true of French-speaking universities. However, there are some differences in approach. In French-speaking cantons, for example, it is common to go from upper secondary education straight to university. The average period of study leading to a master's degree is nine semesters - three semesters short of the average study period in German-speaking Switzerland (Diem 1996). Among other things, the relatively shorter study period in French-speaking cantons can be explained by rigid educational structures and regulations, in contrast to a more liberal approach in German-speaking Switzerland which relies on self-motivation (Galley 1992).

The frequency of on-the-job training and temporary work experience is also different between the two regions. Vocational training alongside theoretical schooling is deeply rooted in Switzerland, particularly in the German-speaking region. This is borne out by statistics which reveal that in German-speaking Switzerland, more than three quarters of students spend a period of gainful employment between the completion of their studies at secondary level II and the beginning of their university-level studies. In Latin regions, only a third of all students benefit from this kind of temporary work experience.

REGIONAL DIFFERENCES IN THE LABOUR MARKET

At a more general level we now examine the situation of young people in the labour market by different regions and across age groups. The comparisons are made on the basis of data drawn from the Swiss Labour Force Survey (SLFS) which has been compiled annually since 1991. These statistics will help us understand, at least quantitatively, some aspects of young people's life. However, the data reveal relatively little about the brief transitionary phase from school to work. The definition of youth is somewhat amended to cover the 15-29 age range since most graduates are older than 25 by the time they complete their studies in higher education. Given the limitation of our data we will concentrate largely on the higher education to work transition.

The economic situation in French- and German-speaking regions and the effect on unemployment

As mentioned previously the average rate of unemployment is significantly lower in the German-speaking part of the country than in the French-speaking region. This difference is difficult to explain, and cannot be attributed solely to respective economic circumstances. On closer inspection it becomes apparent that the differences are in fact structural. Such differences are more pronounced in periods of prosperity than in periods of recession. As for the period under investigation, 1991 to 1996, we can refer to a recent assessment (Kommission für Konjunkturfragen 1996) by the national economic council which states that the economic development of the two language regions has been largely similar, with the exception of only a few industrial sectors.

Employment and unemployment by age and education

Employment and unemployment statistics drawn from the SLFS conform to the recommendations of the International Labour Office (ILO) and the Organisation for Economic Co-operation and Development (OECD), in that they are derived from direct sampling. SLFS statistics also allow us to take a closer look at the respondents' general socio-economic situation, in particular with reference to demographic data. In what follows, these data are complemented by official claimant statistics. The analysis continues to be based on the two main language regions of Switzerland, the German-speaking central and eastern regions, and French-speaking West Switzerland. It should be noted, however, that the cantons of Ticino and Fribourg have been excluded, since the former is Italian-speaking and, until 1996, has had no university, while the latter is a dual-language (French/German) canton.[6]

a. Employment and unemployment

By international standards, present day Switzerland has a high rate of employment and relatively low unemployment. Amongst all Swiss workers it is the young who have the highest risk of being out of work. However, the probability of long unemployment spells is low. It should also be noted that the unemployment rate of young people is very volatile; young workers are the first to be affected by recession but also the first to profit from an economic upswing. Age is thus an important variable and Table 1 shows the rate of employment (REP) and the rate of unemployment (RUP) for both, 15-29 year olds and 30-54 year olds. The latter is used as a means of comparing youth labour markets with labour market conditions for those who are neither concerned by transitions from school to work nor by early retirement.

Table 1
The employment situation by regions and age groups (1992-96)

	DCH 30-54[*]		DCH 15-29		FCH 30-54		FCH 15-29	
	REP	RUP	REP	RUP	REP	RUP	REP	RUP
1992	85.9	1.9	63.0	3.0	81.6	3.5	56.0	7.9
1993	84.3	2.8	62.0	4.0	81.4	4.2	52.6	9.8
1994	84.3	3.0	60.3	3.8	80.4	4.7	52.6	10.4
1995	84.7	2.3	60.1	3.4	82.8	4.3	51.3	9.3
1996	85.6	2.4	59.4	4.0	81.6	4.8	52.8	11.2

Source: Swiss Labour Force Survey, several years and own calculations.

Two things stand out when Table 1 is examined. First, the clear differences between the regions - even at the beginning of the recession - have remained remarkably stable throughout the period in question. Second, the employment rate for the 30-54 age group remains virtually unchanged, both in the German-speaking and the French-speaking areas. The data thus indicates that this age group has not been seriously affected by the recession. It also shows that the deterioration in the labour market has been driven largely by young and old employees. A comparison of the changes in all variables, expressed as percentage proportions, demonstrates that the structural differences at the beginning of the recession have failed to disappear. However, there are no discernible

---

[6] The abbreviation LCH stands for Latin Switzerland and includes the cantons of Fribourg and Ticino. The abbreviation FCH stands for French speaking Switzerland and is used when these two cantons are excluded.

differences in economic development between the regions that are capable of explaining a double-digit unemployment rate among young people in French-speaking Switzerland.

b. Employment situation of first-time job seekers

Another marked difference comes to light when we examine some data on first-time job seekers. In 1996, nearly a quarter of unemployed youth in the French-speaking cantons came directly from the educational system, compared with just 15 per cent of the unemployed in the German-speaking cantons. The difference is particularly pronounced with students in tertiary education, whereas there appears to be no clear regional difference for trainees of the dual education system. This then indicates that even in West Switzerland, graduates of the dual system experience fewer problems, at least when it comes to their transitional path into the labour market. It also suggests that the higher average rate of unemployment in the West may be exacerbated by the fact that a large number of unemployed youth have had no work experience of any kind.

c. Regional comparison of wages

Finally, it is interesting to look into the question of wage differentials which might affect young people who have succeeded in their transition to the labour market. A comparison of average and median wages by age groups, regions and educational levels shows no significant differences. The only noteworthy peculiarity occurs when salaries of university graduates are compared.

The wage curve over a full working life shows that young German-speaking university graduates enter the workforce at a lower wage level - relative to the respective average wage in the region - than their counterparts in West Switzerland. However, with increasing age their salary curve rises more sharply than that of French-speaking graduates. The rise in salary is particularly steep for the 35-39 age group, i.e. at a time when the first career steps have been mastered. Even though the regional differences are relatively small, our observations lead us to two conclusions. First, the wage level in West Switzerland has not fallen, even though unemployment is higher than the national average. This could be due to a lack of wage flexibility, or to "insider-outsider" problems. Second, German-speaking university graduates seem to enjoy a relatively easier access to employment because wage restraints facilitate their entry to the labour market.

3. The employment situation of university graduates

Every two years, the Swiss Working Group for Academic Study and Career Counselling (AGAB) carries out a comprehensive questionnaire-based investigation into the employment situation of graduates from Swiss universities (Diem 1996). On the basis of this evidence, it is possible to compare the employment situation for university graduates in the different language regions (see Table 2).

---

[*] DCH 30-54 = German-speaking Switzerland, and age group 30-54; FCH 30-54 = French-speaking Switzerland, age group 30-54, etc.

Table 2
The employment situation by language region in 1981-1995 (in per cent)

	German-speaking Switzerland			French-speaking West Switzerland		
	Job seekers	REP	Job renunciation rate	Job seekers	REP	Job renunciation rate
1981	2.1	88.1	9.8	2.4	87.8	9.7
1983	4.4	86.7	8.9	6.7	85.7	7.6
1985	3.0	89.5	7.5	6.9	87.5	5.6
1987	2.3	91.5	6.1	4.1	89.3	6.5
1989	2.3	91.4	5.3	4.2	88.2	7.6
1991	3.1	91.7	5.2	8.8	82.7	8.4
1993	7.1	89.0	3.9	13.7	78.4	7.9
1995	4.2	92.4	3.5	10.0	83.8	6.2

Source: Diem (1996)

In recent history the unemployment rate in Latin Switzerland has usually been higher than in the German-speaking part of the country. The latter's average unemployment rate throughout the 1980s amounts to 2.8 per cent, compared with an average of 3.7 per cent in Latin Switzerland. The employment rate has been correspondingly higher in the German-speaking area, albeit only slightly, at just 90 per cent. During the same period, about 7.5 per cent of school-leavers with sufficient qualifications to enter higher education in both parts of the country renounced to enter the labour market. More youngsters in Latin Switzerland than in German-speaking Switzerland stayed on in education. This difference in behaviour is not really surprising if one bears in mind that higher education in Latin Switzerland can be completed relatively quicker than in German-speaking Switzerland.

a. Employment and unemployment during the 1991-95 period of recession

Table 2 shows that between 1991 and 1995 a significant rise in the unemployment rate on both sides of the language divide was witnessed. This increase was far more pronounced in West Switzerland, both in relative and absolute terms. Table 2 also shows that the fall in the employment rate (REP) in the French-speaking region was accordingly greater. At first glance it seems surprising to find that despite economic stagnation the job renunciation rate was falling in German-speaking Switzerland and stable in the French-speaking region. One possible explanation is that in order to safeguard their position in the labour market - particularly at times of an economic crisis - youngsters may deem it necessary to launch their labour market careers as soon as possible after completing their studies.

On the basis of conventional indicators, it seems that the recession has made the situation for youngsters considerably worse in West Switzerland than in other parts of the country. This finding is borne out by the number of new graduates in French-speaking Switzerland who have involuntarily accepted positions of part-time employment during the recession. In fact, the number of involuntary young part-timers trebled to a total of 11.4 per cent , whilst it only doubled in the German-speaking region to reach 7.2 per cent.

b. The quality of employment

Employment statistics tell us nothing about the quality of employment. It is possible that as a result of a recession labour market imbalances force job seekers to consider positions which do not correspond to their educational profile. In both parts of the country a new trend for graduates seems to develop which sees them accepting jobs for which no higher education qualifications are required. During the 1980s, the respective percentage proportions have indeed increased from 12.0 to 14.6 per cent in German-speaking Switzerland, and from 14.8 per cent to 17 per cent in West Switzerland. Since the early 1990s there have been further increases in the two main language regions. In the French-speaking area the figure increased by 1.1 per cent (to 18.1 per cent), in the German-speaking region it has grown by twice that rate. These regional differences may be explained by non-economic factors. For example, unemployment is seen as less of a stigma in French-speaking Switzerland's urban areas. There is correspondingly less social pressure to take a job if the qualification requirement does not match the applicant's educational background.

c. Students and part-time employment

The significance of part-time employment whilst studying varies greatly from one field of study to another. It appears to be particularly useful in disciplines which do not provide the kind of expertise that prepares the student for a specific line of work, including the humanities and the social sciences. Table 3 shows that in 1995 new graduates in these disciplines suffered from an above average rate of unemployment (RUP). However, our analysis also shows that work experience in the form of some part-time work of more than a year has a positive effect on future employment prospects. This effect is particularly visible in German-speaking Switzerland.

Less easy to explain is the surprisingly high level of unemployment among new graduates in the western region of Switzerland who have also gained some work experience during their studies. One possible, yet somewhat controversial explanation is that employers in the region attribute less importance to some qualified professional experience of new graduates than their counterparts in German-speaking Switzerland. The labour market in western Switzerland would thus appear to have more modest expectations with respect to the professional experience of new graduates.

Table 3
**Student employment and the employment chances of students in the humanities
and the social sciences**

Various unemployment ratios	DCH	LCH	DCH index	LCH index	Quotients
	a	b	4.2%=100	10.0%=100	1/a*b
RUP total in %	4.2	10.0	100.0	100.0	2.4
RUP Phil I total in %	5.5	12.0	131.0	120.0	2.2
RUP Phil I with part-time work in %	3.4	10.0	81.0	100.0	2.9
RUP Phil I without part-time work in %	11.4	15.0	271.4	150.0	1.3

Source: Diem (1996) and own calculations

EMPLOYMENT OF NEW GRADUATES IN THE TERTIARY, NON-UNIVERSITY SECTOR

In addition to traditional academic education in universities, tertiary non-university training also plays a significant role in Switzerland's education system. The most important institutions in this context are those which offer both technical and economic training at the highest level. It is for this reason that since 1993 the Federal Office for Economic Development and Labour together with the Swiss Federal Statistical Office has conducted some bi-annual research to investigate the situation of the new graduates of these institutions (Martinez 1996). Here too, the differences between the linguistic regions are remarkable.

a. Employment and unemployment

Not unlike the transition from university-to-work, the transition from non-university tertiary education to employment seems to be more difficult to achieve in Latin Switzerland than in German-speaking Switzerland (see Table 4). The labour market indicators in Table 4 suggest once more that employment problems in the two regions are of a rather different nature.

b. Students and part-time employment

The difference in labour market integration problems on either side of the language divide also appears to be driven by the extent of relevant work experience. German speaking graduates of non-university tertiary institutions generally possess more practical job-related experience than their French-speaking colleagues. Most German-speaking graduates have followed exactly the same upper secondary level path, i.e. an apprenticeship which incorporates on-the-job experience and which lasts longer in

German-speaking Switzerland than in the French-speaking region. In the Germanic area, most students have worked for more than three years before they embark upon post-secondary studies. In the French-speaking region just over 20 per cent of students have benefited from such work experience.

Table 4
The employment situation of non-university students by language region

	DCH			LCH		
	Job-seekers	REP	Job renunciation. r.	Job seekers	REP	Job renunciation r.
1993	6.3	90.0	3.7	22.6	65.9	11.4
1995	3.5	94.0	2.6	10.1	83.1	6.8

Source: Martinez (1996)

CONCLUDING REMARKS

Our analysis points to significant regional differences in the way unemployment affects Swiss youth. We commenced our study with the assumption that these differences can be explained by differences in different education systems in Switzerland. We conclude that a single simple cause does not exist. In fact, our analysis identifies a number of reasons which may lead to youth unemployment or bumpy rides from school to work.

First, the preference for theoretical education in West Switzerland means that the young people there have no contact with the labour market for a considerable period of time. This makes their eventual integration into the labour market more difficult. Although this evidence is important, it is not sufficient to explain all regional differences. After all, almost 50 per cent of the young French-speaking and Italian-speaking Swiss benefit from the dual approach to education. Work experience is of undoubted significance when regional differences are to be explained. Youngsters in German-speaking Switzerland experience considerably more spells of on-the-job training and work than in Western Switzerland. This may take the form of part-time work, the practical training of students, or non-university training for graduates of teachers training schools. Furthermore, both vertical and horizontal flexibility, in particular amongst university graduates, are needed to facilitate entry into the labour market under difficult conditions. Finally, wage expectations also play an important role. Our findings indicate that here too the German-speaking Swiss show slightly more flexibility than their counterparts in Western Switzerland. Although consistent with rational economic behaviour we are unable to demonstrate that French-speaking Swiss price themselves into the labour market by lowering wage demands.

Table 5
Unemployment rates according to fields of study and language regions

Type of education	DCH	LCH	Quotient
	1	2	2/1
Total	3.5	10.0	2.9
Higher college economists	2.5	5.1	2.0
University-educated economists	4.2	10.2	2.4
Higher college engineer	3.7	12.7	3.4
University-educated engineer	5.2	15.7	3.0

Source: Diem (1996), Martinez (1996) and own calculations.

In conclusion, our findings suggest that the knowledge in Switzerland of the factors that govern a successful transition from school to work are rudimentary at best and - in part due to a lack of data - difficult to interpret. Have those in charge of reforming the education system paid sufficient attention to changing circumstances and respective effects on the labour market? We come to the conclusion that they have not. At a time when the providers of education can no longer assume that youngsters will find one job or another, the need to come to terms with dynamic labour market requirements has never been more urgent. However, these assertions are just straws in the wind unless more information is made available - not only labour market information in general but in particular information on this highly critical process of transition from school to work.

REFERENCES

Bundesamt für Statistik (1996), *Bildungsabschlüsse 1995 - Sekundarstufe II und Tertiärstufe*, Bundesamt für Statistik, Bern.

Diem, M. (1996), *Die Beschäftigungssituation der Neuabsolventen der Schweizer Hochschulen 1995*, mimeo.

Wolter, S.C. (1988), *Jugendarbeitslosigkeit*, SVB, Bern

OECD (1996), *Education at a glance - OECD Indicators*, Organisation for Economic Cooperation and Development, Paris.

Galley, F. (1992), *Die Studiendauer an den schweizerischen Hochschulen. Unterschiede und Bestimmungsfaktoren*, Schweizerischer Wissenschaftsrat, Bern.

Kommission für Konjunkturfragen (1996), "Konjunkturentwicklung in der Deutschschweiz, in der Westschweiz und im Tessin", *Beilage zur WirtschaftsPolitik*, vol. 7, pp. 31-34.

Martinez, E. (1996), *Diplomierte der Höheren Fachschulen - Beschäftigungssituation 1995*, Bundesamt für Industrie, Gewerbe und Arbeit und Bundesamt für Statistik. Bern.

PART II

THE ROLE OF TRAINING AND FORMAL QUALIFICATIONS

CHAPTER 5

QUALIFICATIONS AND EMPLOYMENT IN BRITAIN: A LONGITUDINAL ANALYSIS

GARY POLLOCK

INTRODUCTION

The accumulation of qualifications has become a central feature of growing up. As young people progress through the education system they are constantly reminded of the importance of qualifications for future life. The logic is simple: by possessing qualifications one is better placed to gain employment and develop a career. The better these qualifications, the more advantaged one becomes. In such a situation there are winners and losers with the winners having proved their worth in the examination halls. This is, of course, a gross simplification and misrepresentation of the link between qualifications and employment. Indeed there is no necessary link between qualifications and employment. It need only exist where the qualification represents some element of skill or knowledge that has been obtained and is essential within the workplace. Arguably most jobs may now be said to contain sufficient skill requirements to warrant some form of qualification. Furthermore, it is naive to assume that gaining qualifications is an individualised process unconnected with other societal structures, or that after having obtained qualifications there is some sort of natural progression into certain forms of employment (Ashton and Field 1976). As such the questions of interest here focused upon the value of qualifications in relation to employment and thus inevitably touch upon social mobility. While it would be desirable to examine social mobility by comparing origins and destinations it is outside the scope of this paper which instead focuses on destinations in relation to qualifications. Of interest is the extent to which possession and level of qualifications in some way determine occupational outcomes and how this might have changed over the years. Throughout this century the spheres of both education and employment have passed through a number of fundamental changes. These changes have meant that more and more people stay on in education past the minimum school leaving age and gain further qualifications. The labour market has been radically changed such that there is now a much narrower manufacturing base and a much larger service sector. In other words, the population has become more educated and the demands placed upon the workforce have substantially changed. Within this context it is pertinent to study the ways in which qualifications can be seen to have an effect upon employment outcome. Here the employment outcome at age 30 is examined in relation to level and type of qualifications gained.

QUALIFICATIONS AND EMPLOYMENT

The entry into employment and early career development has long been shown to have more to do with opportunities rather than choices (Roberts 1968). Moreover, the choices that do impact upon employment, while containing some elements of rational decision making, are enmeshed with a whole range of life-course issues and an unequal allocation of resources and are thus not reducible to any single factor (Hodkinson and Sparkes 1997). Contemporary society has recently been argued to be becoming more risk fraught and uncertain (Beck 1992) with greater possibilities to exercise choice thus resulting in more individualised biographies. While it can be accepted that young people today do face an uncertain future in relation to employment, partly due to a fragmenting labour market (Pollock 1997), any increase in levels of choice must still be seen as choices within the structural constraints associated with class of origin (Roberts 1995). Indeed the importance of occupational class of origin in determining employment outcome continues to play a vital role in our discussion (Goldthorpe 1987). Education, particularly in the form of qualifications does, however, enter into this relationship and acts as a conduit through which class differences are reproduced (Stewart, Prandy and Blackburn 1980; Bourdieu 1984).

The issue examined here is the relationship between qualifications and employment over time. In particular, the extent to which the possession of a certain level of qualifications can be seen to have an effect on certain employment outcomes as have been found elsewhere (Furlong 1992), and how such effects have changed over the past 60 years. It is thus an examination of destinations, and the role played by qualifications in these destinations. There has been a succession of changes to the education system in Britain, many of which have been a result of, all of which have had an effect on the changes to the labour market. The successive raising of the school leaving age, the expansion of further and higher education have all contributed to the overall increasing significance of education and qualifications. Most recently, the 'New Vocationalism' has been formulated as a response to a perceived 'skills gap' whereby young people are said to be unequipped to enter into the contemporary labour market.

DATA

The BHPS[7] is a nationally representative survey which has visited a panel of approximately 10,000 people every year since 1991 and questioned them on their socio-economic status and various socio-economic issues. In 1993 panel members were also asked to describe their lifetime employment histories and it is this data which is used here. The data is thus retrospectively longitudinal, with older respondents being required to recall events taking place over 40 years ago. Despite this, a review of the literature on the reliability of recall data shows that summary details of employment histories can be collected with a reasonable degree of accuracy (Dex 1991). Gershuny and Brice (1994) further note that employment history recall has a constant level of reliability. The management of longitudinal data of this sort is notoriously complex. Work carried out on the Social Change and Economic Life Initiative has been invaluable in dealing with these complexities (Marsh and Gershundy 1991) as have been the BHPS manuals produced by the ESRC Centre on Micro-social Change at the University of Essex (Taylor 1996a, 1996b).

AGE, PERIOD AND COHORT

Longitudinal data is rich and makes it possible for the analyst to examine data in relation to three important variables, that of age, period and cohort. *Age* refers to the age of the individual - this obviously varies for each individual over time in a longitudinal survey but it is, for example, possible to calculate the proportion of men or women in a particular occupational category at the age of 30. Such a statistic is of limited use, however, as there is no control over the point in time (*period*) at which these people were employed full-time. It is essential to have some knowledge when particular events have occurred in order to provide necessary explanatory information with which to contextualize the findings (Davies 1994). For example a 30 year old today faces a very different labour market to a 30 year old during the 1960s. *Cohort* refers to a group of individuals of a similar age during the same period. Analysing longitudinal data using cohorts facilitates the comparison of groups of people of a similar age but at different periods. It is thus an effective means of highlighting changes over time by separating age and period effects.

The sample was subdivided into decennial birth cohorts in order to facilitate a comparative analysis between people born in the different decades (Gershuny and Brice (1994) discuss this process). Table 1 shows the sample characteristics for each of the birth cohorts. Aggregation into cohorts will inevitably reduce the precision with which period effects can be attributed to a particular year as a result of grouping such a wide age range.

---

[7] The data used in this paper were made available through The Data Archive. The data were originally collected by the ESRC Research Centre on Micro-social Change at the University of Essex. Neither the original collectors of the data nor the Archive bear any responsibility for the analyses or interpretations presented here.

For example, the year in which the people from the 1920s cohort had their 30th birthday ranges from 1950 to 1959. Greater precision could be attained by using narrower birth cohorts. It was, however, felt that broad changes in employment would be discernible and more easily interpreted from decennial cohorts. Nonetheless there is a distinct danger that period effects may be diluted so far as to render them unidentifiable. Thus any cyclical changes in the labour market are likely to be underestimated. The relationship between birth cohort and the range at which they are aged 30 is shown in the final column of table 1. It should, however, be noted that the 1960s birth cohort is not fully covered by this period. A person born in 1969, for example, is 24 in 1993 hence this cohort is incomplete, only recording data for people born up to 1963. Finally, the life history data was recorded such that a person could only possess one event type at any one point in time. It was thus impossible, for example, for the data to record a person with two jobs at the same time. Respondents are thus forced to choose one job to represent their main form of employment. This presents problems when interpreting the data. It does however, make the data management a much simpler task.

Table 1: Decennial birth cohorts broken down by sex.

Birth Cohort	Men	Women	All	Range when aged 30
1910s	210	367	577	1940-49
1920s	468	578	1,046	1950-59
1930s	518	569	1,087	1960-69
1940s	770	882	1,652	1970-79
1950s	831	887	1,718	1980-89
1960s	305	327	632	1990-99[a]
All	3,159	3,699	6,858	

[a] this birth cohort only contains data for those aged 30 up until 1993

Here, the relationship between qualification and employment variables is examined to illustrate the changing nature of this link over the years[8]. The employment variables refer to the employment situation for each respondent at the age of 30. Employment at the age of 30 is used in an attempt to provide an analysis in relation to what could be argued to be each person's occupational career. There are, of course, problems with this assumption but it does serve to allow for some horizontal and vertical movement at the early stages of people's careers and thus hopefully represents a more stable period of

---

[8] While it would have been desirable to link employment and qualification directly, for example by identifying when a qualification was obtained this was not possible. The retrospective employment history data does contain information on exactly when jobs were experienced but there was no such collection of retrospective qualifications data. Thus what is used here is qualifications as achieved by the date of the survey (1993).

employment when compared with, for example, the first job on leaving full time education.

Figure 1: Highest qualification by birth cohort, women

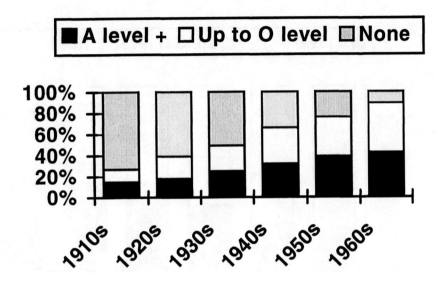

RESULTS

The analysis concentrates on two qualification variables and five employment variables; highest educational qualification (including non-academic qualifications) and whether or not the respondent holds a vocational qualification. Employment was examined in relation to firstly the occupational classification[9] , secondly whether or not the job was full-time, thirdly whether or not the contract was permanent, fourthly the length of the job (this could actually extend beyond age 30), and lastly how many different jobs had been done by the age of 30. In choosing employment outcome at the

---

[9] The International (ISCO-88) classification of occupations was used and re-coded into five categories as follows;

Category 1 comprises ISCO-88 Major Groups 1 and 2. Legislators, senior officials managers and professionals.

Category 2 comprises ISCO-88 Major Group 3. Technicians and associate professionals.

Category 3 comprises ISCO-88 Major Group 4. Clerks.

Category 4 comprises ISCO-88 Major Group 5. Service workers and shop and market sales workers.

Category 5 comprises ISCO-88 Major Groups 7,8 and 9. Craft and related trade workers, plant and machine operators, assemblers, and elementary occupations.

ISCO-88 Major Groups 6 and 10 (skilled agricultural and fishery workers, and armed forces) were not used due to the problems they pose in occupational schema's (Esping-Andersen 1993).

age of 30 each person can be said to have 'arrived' in their career. As such the problems associated with young workers being restricted as a result of age structured labour markets is overcome (Ashton, Maguire and Garland 1982).[10]

Figure 2: Highest qualification, men

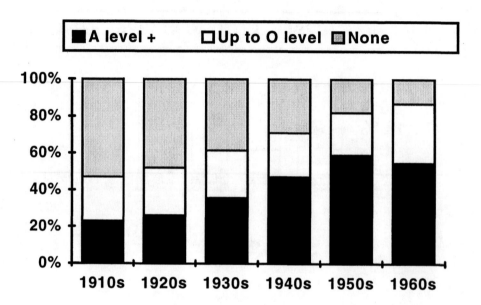

Figures one and two confirm that there has been a rise in credentialisation for both women and men throughout the century with only around 10% of both women and men from the 1960s cohort with no qualifications. While the pattern is similar for both women and men it is clear that increases in A level and above qualifications among women are slower than for men (although levels actually fell for the 1960s cohort) with larger gains being made in the 'up to O level' category.

Again, when examining the possession of vocational qualifications over the years the pattern is virtually identical for both women and men, the only noticeable difference being the higher level among men, although the gap has all but closed. Undoubtedly the various Youth and Employment Training initiatives have served to increase overall levels of vocational qualifications and have also perhaps been responsible for increasing the relative proportion of women with such qualifications.

The scene is thus set in which as the years go by, more and more people gain more and more qualifications with the obvious problem that unless the number of jobs increases, there is inevitably greater competition for the jobs which remain.

---

[10] It will, however, be useful to incorporate some measure of employment biography into the analysis in the future, to examine the theses in relation to age structured labour markets.

Turning to employment, Table 2 shows the occupational structure of women and men with jobs at the age of 30 broken down by birth cohort. It is clear that for both women and men the 'senior and professional' category increases in size for the 1940s birth cohort (these people were thus aged 30 somewhere between 1970 and 1979) and remains as large. The 'technical and associated' category increases only marginally for both women and men throughout the years. Both the category 'clerks' and 'service, shop and sales' are invariably three times as large for women than for men, although there are signs that this difference may be falling. Finally, the 'craft, plant and elementary occupations' category is steadily declining for both women and men over the years, with women showing larger rates of decline. The fundamental changes in the structure of the labour market which have taken place since the end of the second world war are thus reflected in the data.

Table 2: Occupational classification of women and men at age 30 by birth cohort.

	1910s	1920s	1930s	1940s	1950s	1960s
Women	%	%	%	%	%	%
Senior and professional	9	7	9	14	14	14
Technical and associated	7	8	12	8	12	12
Clerks	22	30	31	34	32	31
Service, shop and sales	18	20	17	21	24	25
Craft, plant, elementary	45	36	31	24	18	18
N	(268)	(489)	(487)	(748)	(753)	(224)
Men	%	%	%	%	%	%
Senior and professional	17	12	13	22	24	22
Technical and associated	5	8	13	12	11	12
Clerks	13	12	9	9	9	12
Service, shop and sales	8	6	5	7	6	8
Craft, plant, elementary	56	61	60	50	50	46
N	(174)	(379)	(414)	(583)	(622)	(187)

Having identified changes in the occupational structure and a general increase in numbers gaining qualifications for both men and women the key question is the extent to which there have been any changes in the relationship between these two variables. Table 3 shows the joint distribution of qualifications and occupation by both birth cohort and sex. Most notable is that for all occupational groups there has been a marked decline in levels of non-qualification. There is thus evidence that there is a loosening of the link between qualifications and occupation such that level of qualification may be less good at predicting occupational category than it used to be. Despite the changes in level and distribution of qualifications they do still seem to represent quite consistent predictors of occupational outcome with a few exceptions. While it is difficult establishing a clear pattern from a table with this many cells[11] there are important differences between women and men. In particular it can be discerned that in most occupational categories across most cohorts there are larger percentages of men than women in the 'A level and above' and categories. This shows that at this level of aggregation[12] men are on average better qualified than women throughout the occupational structure.

Figure 3: % of men and women with vocational qualification

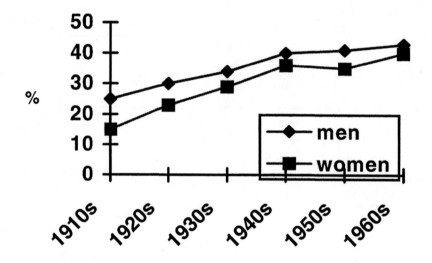

---

[11] In fact a logistic regression with occupational category as a multinomial outcome is currently being produced to facilitate a more thorough analysis of this data.

[12] The level of aggregation of both occupation and qualification are potential areas of concern when the cell counts get quite low. An alternative approach would be to use the Cambridge scales instead of occupational groupings in analysing differences between qualification categories.

Table 3: Occupation at age 30 and education by birth cohort, women and men

		1910s	1920s	1930s	1940s	1950s	1960s
Women		%	%	%	%	%	%
Senior and prof	A level and above	55	81	79	72	86	78
	Up to O level	9	10	12	17	8	13
	None	36	10	9	10	6	9
	N	(22)	(31)	(43)	(105)	(107)	(32)
Technical and assoc	A level and above	53	76	67	72	65	70
	Up to O level	16	11	21	18	27	26
	None	32	13	12	10	8	4
	N	(19)	(38)	(57)	(60)	(92)	(27)
Clerks	A level and above	19	17	21	24	29	33
	Up to O level	29	48	47	58	59	65
	None	52	35	32	18	12	1
	N	(58)	(145)	(152)	(251)	(241)	(69)
Service, shop and sales	A level and above	4	6	11	20	34	30
	Up to O level	9	9	16	32	35	61
	None	87	85	73	47	31	9
	N	(46)	(98)	(82)	(154)	(176)	(56)
Craft, plant, elementary	A level and above	3	2	4	15	6	18
	Up to O level	6	10	10	19	30	50
	None	91	87	86	66	64	33
	N	(119)	(175)	(148)	(175)	(135)	(40)
Men		%	%	%	%	%	%
Senior and prof	A level and above	75	60	71	84	89	80
	Up to O level	4	24	16	7	9	15
	None	21	15	14	9	2	5
	N	(28)	(45)	(51)	(128)	(151)	(41)
Technical and assoc	A level and above	44	64	58	64	81	91
	Up to O level	33	16	15	28	16	9
	None	22	19	27	8	3	0
	N	(9)	(31)	(55)	(72)	(70)	(23)
Clerks	A level and above	27	28	47	52	59	59
	Up to O level	23	30	33	31	28	18
	None	50	41	19	17	13	23
	N	(22)	(46)	(36)	(52)	(54)	(22)
Service, shop and sales	A level and above	21	9	10	38	58	47
	Up to O level	21	26	25	30	24	47
	None	57	65	65	33	18	6
	N	(14)	(23)	(20)	(40)	(38)	(15)
Craft, plant, elementary	A level and above	8	16	23	28	38	32
	Up to O level	29	28	30	29	30	46
	None	63	56	47	43	31	21
	N	(100)	(231)	(248)	(290)	(307)	(84)

Unsurprisingly, Table 4 and Figure 4 show declining proportions of full-time employment and permanent contracts for both men and women. For women, this decline is explained by rising proportions of part-time employment and for men by self-employment. When analysed along with qualifications there was no clear pattern suggesting that tenure of employment is unrelated to level of qualifications.

Table 4: Employment status at age 30 by birth cohort

	1910s	1920s	1930s	1940s	1950s	1960s
Women	%	%	%	%	%	%
Full-time	82	82	77	69	65	64
Self	4	1	4	5	4	6
Part-time	14	17	20	27	31	31
N	(270)	(492)	(487)	(749)	(756)	(249)
Men	%	%	%	%	%	%
Full-time	92	94	91	91	85	81
Self	7	6	8	9	14	16
Part-time	1	1	1	*	1	2
N	(183)	(391)	(426)	(601)	(633)	(207)

* less than 0.5%

Figure 4: % of working men and women without a permanent contract by the age of 30

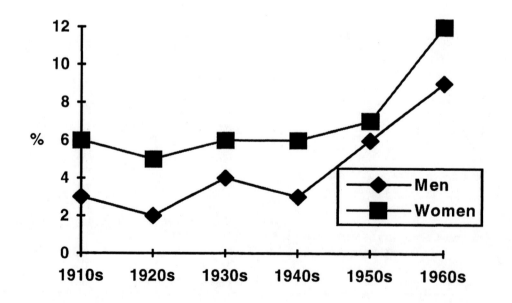

Figure 5 shows the median length of job at age 30 to be falling substantially for men but only gradually for women over the years. While there will be an element of 'right censoring' whereby members of later birth cohorts may still be doing a job which may last for some time in the future there is also the possibility that the average length of job spell is decreasing. When analysed along with qualifications there was no association, suggesting that this is a factor common to all occupational categories. This point is further developed below in an analysis of number of jobs done by the age of 30.

Figure 5: Median length of job at age 30 by sex

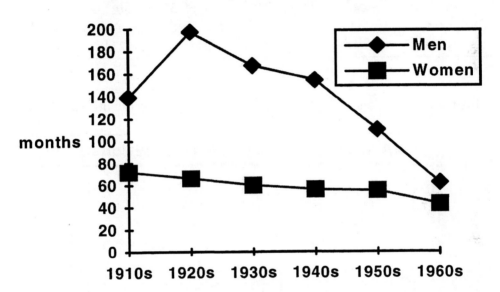

A certain amount of employment mobility is to be expected given that employment at age 30 is being examined. Table 5 shows that for both men and women the number of jobs done by the age of 30 is increasing. This trend could be considered to be negative, possibly a reflection of insecurity in the labour market. It could also be positive showing increased opportunities and possibly even choices in employment. Related work (Pollock 1996, 1998) provides further evidence for the increasing number of employment states experienced by people born in the 1950s and 1960s.

Table 5: Number of different jobs by the age of 30

	1910s	1920s	1930s	1940s	1950s	1960s
Women	%	%	%	%	%	%
one or two	63	55	51	42	37	33
three +	38	46	49	58	64	67
N	(272)	(495)	(490)	(753)	(761)	(273)
Men	%	%	%	%	%	%
one - two	56	42	41	37	35	30
three +	44	58	59	63	65	71
N	(183)	(396)	(431)	(604)	(641)	(224)

Figure 6: Percentages of '3+ jobs' minus '1 or 2 jobs' by qualifications, women

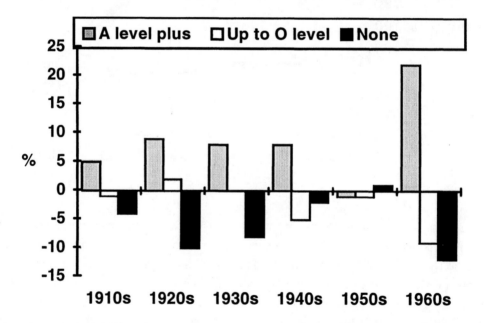

Figures 6 and 7 throw more light upon the trend towards the increasing number of jobs done by the age of 30. These figures show for each category of qualification the difference between the '3+' and the '1 or 2' categories. Thus, where there is little difference the cluster of bars will be small, for example for women in the 1950s. These figures show an interesting difference between women and men. For women, frequent job changers are more likely to be well qualified whereas for men, frequent job changers are more likely to have no qualifications. The explanation could be that women with qualifications can change job or re-enter the labour market after an absence more easily than those without qualifications and that women without qualifications are finding it more difficult to do so. That it is the unqualified men who are the more frequent job changers serves to highlight a key difference between labour market experiences of men and women. A further analysis shows that most of the male frequent job changers occupy the craft, plant, elementary category whereas there is a more even spread of frequent job changers among all the occupational groups for the women.

Figure 7: Percentages of '3+ jobs' minus '1 or 2 jobs' by qualifications, men

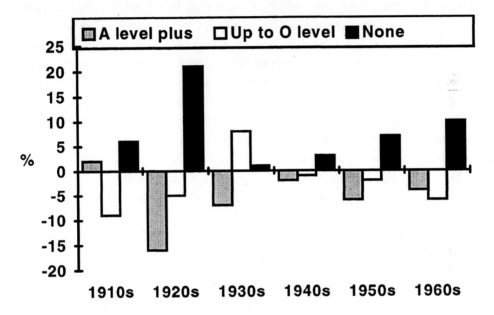

CONCLUDING REMARKS

This Chapter presents results of a preliminary analysis of aspects of the relationship between qualifications and employment using the retrospective life history data from the BHPS. There is still much work to do to in terms of refining the method of analysis to incorporate more aspects of the longitudinal nature of the data. There is also a need to include data on social origins such that questions of inter-generational social mobility can be directly addressed. Conspicuous by its absence here is a multivariate analysis of the data in which employment at outcome is regressed (as a multinomial) with the education and cohort factors. Despite these shortcomings, however, there are some findings of relevance. The increasing credentialisation of the workforce is clearly shown and, more importantly, workers in the occupational categories such as 'craft, plant and elementary' and 'service, shop and sales' are increasingly likely to be well qualified as the years have gone by (Table 3). It cannot be ascertained from this data whether the possession of qualifications is becoming more of a necessity for these occupations in terms of required skill or learning, neither can it be shown that qualifications are being used when selecting job applicants more than in the past. It is, however, highly likely that with increasing credentialisation that qualifications are being used in the applications process. As such competition for jobs in the occupations noted above has become increasingly based upon possession of more and better qualifications than previously. Moreover, there is also evidence that male workers are generally more qualified than females throughout the occupational categories. A crude measure of job mobility - the number of different jobs by the age of 30 - shows women, unsurprisingly, to have higher rates. More interesting is that women frequent job changers are better qualified than men frequent job changers (Figures 6 and 7). This seems to be related to occupational category such that men who change job frequently are concentrated in the 'craft, plant, elementary' category, whereas women who change jobs frequently are more evenly spread among all the occupational categories. In short, an occupation at age 30 appears to have been linked to qualifications throughout the post war period although the relationship has been steadily changing as a result of increasing credentialisation and changes in the occupational structure. The possession of qualifications has become more closely linked with all occupational categories. There is still, however, a hierarchical relationship between qualifications and occupation such that good qualifications remain more closely associated with 'senior, professional' and 'technical and associate professions' than with the other categories.

REFERENCES

Ashton, D.N. and Field, D. (1976), *Young Workers,* London: Hutchinson.

Roberts, K. (1968), "The entry into employment: an approach towards a general theory", *Sociological Review,* vol. 16, pp165-184.

Hodkinson, P. and Sparkes, A. C. (1997), "Careership: a sociological theory of career decision making", *British Journal of Sociology of Education,* vol. 18, no 1, pp29-44.

Beck, U. (1992), *Risk Society*, London: Sage.

Pollock, G. (1997), "Individualisation and the transition from youth to adulthood", *Young,* vol. 5, no. 1, pp55-68.

Roberts, K. (1995), *Youth and Employment in Modern Britain*, Oxford: Oxford University Press.

Goldthorpe, J. H. (1987), *Social Mobility and Class Structure in Modern Britain,* 2nd edition, Oxford: Clarendon Press.

Stewart, A., Prandy, K. and Blackburn (1980), *Social Stratification and Occupations*, London: Macmillan.

Bourdieu, P. (1984), *Distinction: A Social Critique of the Judgement of Taste*, London: Routledge and Kegan Paul.

Furlong, A. (1992), *Growing up in a classless society?*, Edinburgh, Edinburgh University Press.

Dex, S. (1991), "The Reliability of Recall Data: A Literature Review", *Working Papers of the ESRC Research Center on Micro-social Change,* Paper 11, Colchester: University of Essex.

Gershuny, J. and Brice, J. (1994), "Looking Backwards: Family and Work 1900 to 1992" in N. Buck, J. Gershuny, D. Rose, and J. Scott (eds), *Changing Households: The British Household Panel Survey 1990-1992,* Essex: ESRC Research Centre on Micro-Social Change.

Marsh, C. and Gershuny, J. (1991), "Handling work history data in standard statistical packages" in S. Dex (ed.), *Life and Work History Analysis: Qualitative and Quantitative Developments,* London: Routledge.

Taylor, M.F. (ed.) (1996a), *British Household Panel Survey User Manual Volume A: Introduction, Technical Report and Appendices,* Colchester: University of Essex.

Taylor, M.F. (ed.) (1996b), *British Household Panel Survey User Manual Volume B: Codebook,* Colchester: University of Essex.

Davies, R. (1994), "From Cross-Sectional to Longitudinal Analysis", in A. Dale and R. Davies (eds.), *Analyzing Social and Political Change: A Casebook of Methods,* London: Sage.

Ashton, D.N., Maguire, M.J. and Garland, V. (1982), *Youth in the Labour Market,* Research Paper No. 34, London: Department of Employment.

Esping-Andersen, G. (1993), "Post-industrial class structures: an analytical framework" in G. Esping-Andersen (ed.), *Changing Classes: stratification and mobility in post-industrial societies,* London: Sage.

Pollock, G. (1997), "Uncertain futures: young people in and out of employment since 1940" paper presented at the British Sociological Association conference, University of Reading.

CHAPTER 6

SCHOOL-TO-WORK TRANSITION AND OCCUPATIONAL CAREERS - RESULTS FROM A LONGITUDINAL STUDY IN GERMANY

UDO KELLE AND JENS ZINN

INTRODUCTION

The transition from the educational system to the labour market in Germany is traditionally linked to the Dual System of *"Vocational Education and Training"* (VET). This system fosters meritocratic access to labour market positions and is based on credentials and formal qualifications. In this chapter it will be shown how this educational institution (together with the school system) guides, controls and influences the occupational life course of young adults until their mid-twenties. For this purpose empirical results will be presented from a panel study which collected longitudinal data about the job entry of young adults in six of the top training occupations in the service and technical industrial sector.

The analysis will commence with some quantitative results which demonstrate the strong influence of gender and social origin on the access to training in a particular occupation. This influence is mediated through the German three tier school system which transforms (but also mitigates) ascriptive properties into social and occupational status. Furthermore, our results demonstrate the long-term influence of the occupation trained for on the life course. Different occupations are not only linked to different social prestige and career opportunities. They are also connected to the differences in the risk of job insecurity and short term employment. Success and difficulties in the first years of the occupational life course are highly dependent on the kind of training offered.

Our analysis continues with some theoretical and methodological background of our research focusing on the relation between agency and structure in the life course. The role of different types of theoretical assumptions in sociological reasoning about the occupational life course will be discussed, and these theoretical questions will be linked to the methodological question of how qualitative and quantitative methods can be integrated.

Some semi-structured qualitative interviews have been used to determine the role of action orientations in the occupational life course. We follow a two-step process to analyse these data: In a first step, we focus on how respondents subjectively interpret and perceive the opportunities and constraints connected with their educational and occupational options and circumstances. Some results of this stage of analysis help us develop "*ethnographies of occupational life worlds*". In a second step we try to identify specific patterns of biographical action orientations by comparing the respondents´ aspirations and interpretations of situations over some years of their life course. In the qualitative data material we discovered six different modes of biographical coping which we call "*biographical action orientations*".

Our statistical data as well as the qualitative results demonstrate the "loose coupling" between the school systems, institutions of the VET, the labour market and the respondents' modes of coping. Moving along a certain occupational pathway results from an interplay between structural and individual aspirations and competencies.

INFLUENCES OF INSTITUTIONS OF THE GERMAN EDUCATION SYSTEM ON THE OCCUPATIONAL LIFE COURSE

In the 1990s two thirds of all school leavers in Germany still enter a three year apprenticeship in the Dual System of Vocational Education and Training (VET). The German apprentice has a specific social status: not yet a junior worker, but a skilled worker in the making, who does not receive wages, but a training allowance, and follows an institutionalised sequence of training under the supervision of teachers and master craftsmen. The curricula are supervised by both the school administration and the chambers of commerce, crafts and industry.

If the role of VET institutions from a sociological life course perspective are examined, questions arise on how this system mediates social stratification in terms of social class as well as stratification in terms of gender differences. Does the system reinforce or weaken the intergenerational reproduction of social inequality or gender differences? And does it promote social mobility of men and women with different class backgrounds?

In order to get a full picture of the entire status passage from school to the labour market, we conducted a panel study in two German cities - Bremen and Munich (Heinz 1996a, 1996b; Heinz, Kelle, Witzel and Zinn 1997). From the top ten training occupations we selected two crafts occupations (hairdressing and car mechanics), two administrative occupations (bank employees and office workers), one technical-industrial occupation (industrial mechanics) and one service sector occupation (retail sales). In 1989 we then interviewed a sample of young apprentices who had started vocational training three years earlier. Two more waves of standardised questionnaires were conducted in 1991 and 1994, respectively. This quantitative study was set up to collect sociodemographic information and event history data about the respondents' occupational life course. From the large quantitative sample a smaller subsample was drawn and qualitative (semi-structured) interviews were conducted. These interviews focused on the respondents' work experiences, their aspirations and reflections on their occupational careers.

Statistical analyses of the quantitative panel data show that there are strong relations between access to training in particular occupations on the one hand and both the school level attainment and the sex of respondents on the other. Two occupations (industrial mechanics and car mechanics) are almost exclusively dominated by male apprentices, while 87 per cent of all sampled hairdressers are female. 82 per cent of office staff and 60 per cent of retail sales persons are female. The only occupation with a reasonable degree of gender-neutrality appears to be that of a bank clerk with 54% male and 46 % female employees (see Figure 1).

There is a strong correlation between entry level education and the occupation trained for. The access to white collar occupations, such as banking and office work, tends to be restricted to the most qualified school leavers from *Realschule* (a school that provides an intermediary school leaving certificate after 10 years) and *Gymnasium* (which pupils leave after 13 years of schooling with the *Abitur* and the opportunity to enter Higher Education). Less qualified young people who have graduated from *Hauptschule* (schooling with a duration of 9 years) are referred to apprenticeships in the trade, crafts and industrial domain (see Figure 2).

There is no reason to doubt that the three tier school system reflects to a high degree the class structure of German society (see also Blossfeld, 1993; Blossfeld and Shavit, 1993). At the *Gymnasium* we find a much higher proportion of pupils with a middle class and upper-middle class family background than at the *Hauptschule*. Social class origin also exerts an influence on the respondent´s decision for a certain training occupation. However, if we model the combined influence of class and school level attainment on occupational choice with the help of a binary logit analysis (see Table 1) we can see that the influence of family background is mediated through gender and school level attainment. Once a son or a daughter of a upper-middle class professional background has entered the *Hauptschule* their chances to become later a bank apprentice is very low.

Figure 1: Distribution of men and women in different occupations

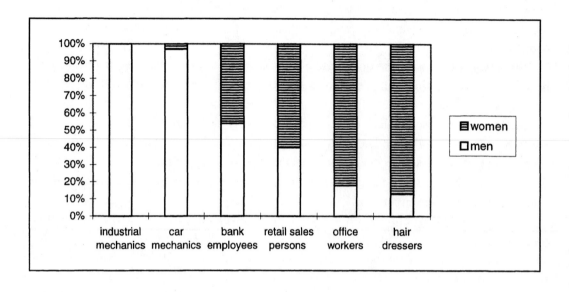

Figure 2: Distribution of school level attainments in six occupations

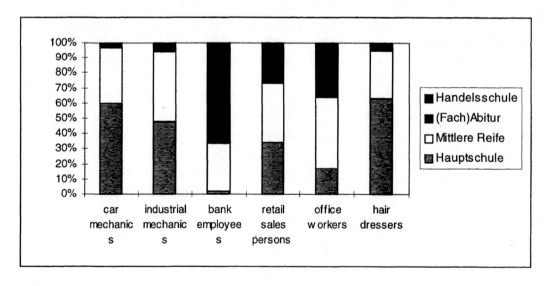

Table 1: Influence of the family's social background and school level attainment on vocational choice of bank employees and industrial mechanics

Category	Explaining variables	coeff	p(T-test)
Bank employees (reference group: others)	*Constant* *sociodemographic status of father* (ref.group: others)	-1,58	<0,0001
	skilled manual worker	-0,64	0,07
	higher grade prof.	0,50	0,007
	school level attainment (ref.group.: Mittl.Reife)		
	Hauptschule	-2,26	<0,0001
	(Fach-)Abitur	1,34	<0,0001
Industrial mechanics (reference group: others)	*Constant* *sociodemographic status of father*	-1,62	<0,0001
	skilled manual worker	0,74	0,003
	higher grade prof.	0,45	0,03
	school level attainment		
	Hauptschule	0,57	0,002
	(Fach-)Abitur	-2,11	<0,0001

Our results demonstrate that the entrance into vocational education and training is socially structured. But how does VET mediate structural influence and thus influence social inequality *over the life course*? To compare the occupational careers of our sample we differentiate between the following five occupational states:

1. *still in occupation* trained for, or in an occupation similar to the occupation trained for
2. working in *another occupation*
3. *returned to school* in order to recover missing formal qualifications, or attending any other form of further education (except higher education)
4. enrolled in *full time technical college* or *university education*
5. *not in the labour force* (without job, on sick leave, pregnant, maternity leave, imprisonment, abroad, military service)

By comparing the occupational status of our respondents four years after completing vocational training some remarkable differences can be observed. The occupation with the most stable career pattern is that of office work (see Figure 3). Only a very small proportion works in another occupation or attends school or colleges to invest in further educational capital.

Figure 3: Occupational developments of office workers

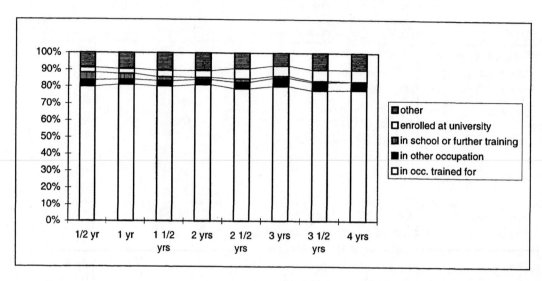

Unlike office workers we find a substantial and growing migration out of the occupation trained for among car mechanics and hairdressers (see Figures 4 and 5). These developments already commence in the first year of their labour market participation. Four years after completing their vocational training more than one third work in another occupation. However, there are also very few car mechanics and hairdressers who have tried to achieve further educational qualifications during the first four years of their occupational life course.

Figure 4: Occupational developments of car mechanics

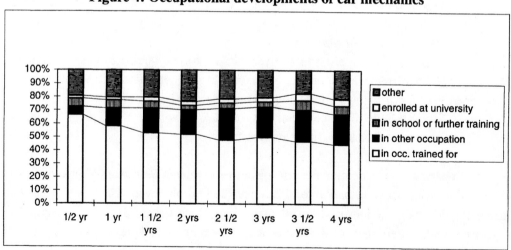

Figure 5: Occupational developments of hairdressers

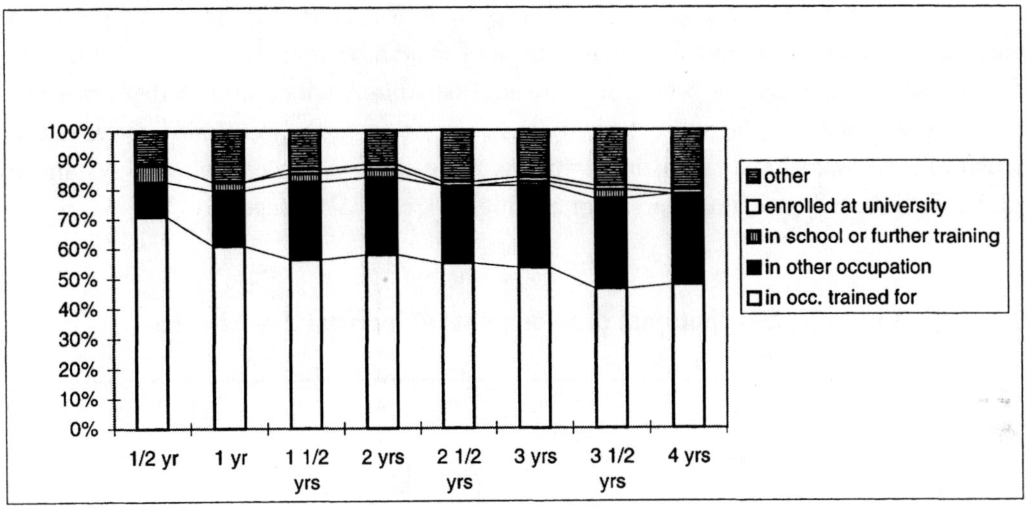

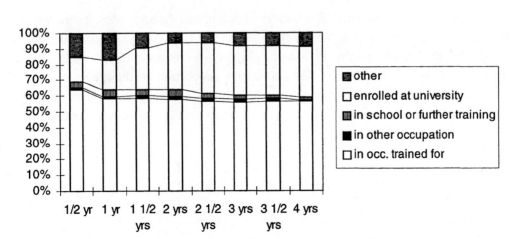

Compared to other occupations the bank employee shows a high tendency to reenter the educational system to invest in their human capital (see Figure 6). Almost immediately after vocational training is completed a considerable number of bank employees leave their job to attend university. Following their military service a third of male bank employees go to university, most of them studying law, economics or business studies.

Figure 6: Occupational developments of bank employees

The most remarkable career patterns are shown by the industrial mechanics. As with hairdressers and car mechanics there is also a large proportion of industrial mechanics who leave their occupation. However, whilst most hairdressers and car mechanics tend to simply change occupations a considerable proportion of industrial mechanics reenter the educational system. As Figure 7 indicates, most of them have to go back to school first in order to achieve the highest school level exam, the *Abitur*, which allows them to enter university. 4 years after the apprenticeship has come to an end, almost one quarter of the industrial mechanics have taken the strenuous route through the educational system in order to achieve a degree at university or at a higher technical college.

Figure 7: Occupational developments of industrial mechanics

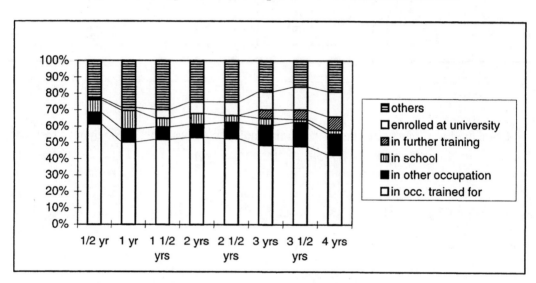

By modeling the influence of school level attainment, father's socio-economic status and occupation trained for on the occupational status four years after the apprenticeship we see that the high proportion of bank employees who return to the educational system can be explained mainly by the fact that a high proportion of them had achieved the *Abitur*. This, however, is not true for the industrial mechanic, where the tendency for further education is independent of the level of attainment at school (see Table 2).

Table 2: Influence of occupation, social origin and school level attainment on university attendance 4 years after vocational training

Category	explaining variables	Coeff.	p. (T-test)
Enrolled in university or college *(reference group: others)*	*Constant*	-1,91	<0,0001
	sociodemographic status of father *(ref.group: lower grade white collar worker)*		
	skilled manual worker	-0,25	0,48
	unskilled manual worker	-0,32	0,39
	higher grade proff.	0,10	0,67
	self employed	0,06	0,83
	school level attainment *(reference group: others)* (Fach-)Abitur	1,17	>0,0001
	occupation *(ref.group: retail sales person)* bank employees	0,44	0,16
	office workers	-0,33	0,30
	industrial mechanics	**0,79**	**0,02**
	car mechanics	0,45	0,28
	hairdresser	-0,50	0,40

There are also a variety of gender differences concerning the occupational status four years after the apprenticeship: more women than men are still working in the occupation trained for, and more men than women are in further schooling or training or attend university. The most meaningful differences can be found if mixed gender occupations are examined. A higher proportion of female than male bank employees remain in their occupation, whilst in retail sales a higher proportion of women than men leave their occupation (see Figure 8). As for bank employees this can be explained through a greater proportion of men in our population with Abitur (50 per cent) entering university than is the case for women (30 per cent). However, among retail sales staff there are more females who enter university (7 per cent) than males (2 per cent).

Figure 8: Distribution of men and women who remained in their occupation in gender-mixed occupations

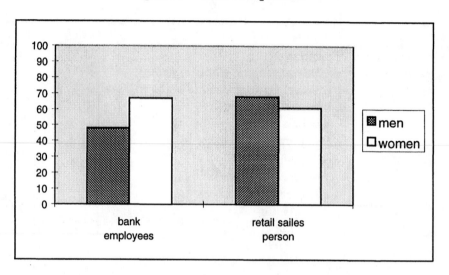

THE COMPLEX INTERPLAY OF AGENCY AND STRUCTURE IN THE OCCUPATIONAL LIFE COURSE

Many differences between occupational groups are easy to interpret if other sociodemographic attributes of the respondents are taken into account. That a high proportion of bank employees, for instance, have taken the route to university is clearly a result of their high school level certification before they entered their vocational training. However, what is remarkable and runs, at least at a first glance, against the assumption of systematic reproduction of social inequality are the 24 per cent of industrial mechanics who went back to school to improve their education and then moved on to university. The results on gender differentiation also require further consideration. Why is the proportion of females leaving their occupation higher among retail sales persons than among bank employees or office workers?

In our research the use of qualitative interviews turned out to be extremely helpful to answer such questions and to guide the interpretation of statistical analysis. As with other forms of sociological research it is also a common fact in life course research that social phenomena found on the aggregate level can only adequately be understood if one refers to "*local knowledge*" of the actors in the empirical field under investigation. To discern such local knowledge, strategies of qualitative data collection through fieldwork and open interviewing, are most appropriate.

Although a considerable amount of methodological writing exists to highlight such issues as "triangulation" and "mixed methods approaches" (see, for instance, Creswell 1994; Flick 1992; Fielding and Fielding 1986; Denzin 1977) the integration of qualitative and quantitative data collection and data analysis strategies can be rarely regarded as a simple methodological task. Qualitative and quantitative researchers often consider themselves as members of different "camps", with different theoretical and methodological backgrounds, with different research domains, and with differing understandings of the nature of social life. Therefore, we will first discuss some theoretical and methodological aspects of the integration of quantitative and qualitative life course data, before presenting some of the results from our qualitative panel study that help transform the statistical results into "rich" descriptions and explanations of social phenomena.

Quantitative life course researchers usually make sense of statistical micro-data by postulating functional relations between variables that denote certain attributes of individuals, including their sex, their occupation trained for, their occupational status some years after they left school or the socio-economic status of their father. Some of these variables are used as independent variables and others as dependent variables. In order to find a sociological interpretation of such a functional relation the independent variable is usually regarded as representing a structural influence on the life course, and the dependent variable as representing the result of actions that are influenced by structural phenomena.

Two main discourses or theoretical approaches in life course research (cf. Heinz 1992) can be used to establish a link between empirical data and theoretical categories. The first approach is mainly concerned with questions of social structure. The second approach places a stronger emphasis on concepts of human agency.

As for the former, using a more structural approach towards the study of the life course proposes that transitions are linked to institutions which structure biographical sequences such as careers. These institutions, as culturally consolidated systems of order, are often formalised in organisations like schools or the VET. These organisations not only reproduce the social structure of society, but also "carry with them the incorporated norms, like a snail carrying its house" (Krueger, 1996).

As for the latter, proponents of a stronger emphasis on human agency would criticise the structural approach for assuming that the life course is a socially organised flow chart that does not take into account the fact that individuals have to make decisions at each turning point. Life course patterns, they would argue, cannot be set in motion without actors who establish a biographically meaningful relationship to institutionalised requirements. Consequently, this approach attempts to interpret the life course from the perspective of the actor, seeing it as a series of selections from institutionalised options (cf. Heinz 1992).

Regardless of the merits of both approaches a gap in the chain of arguments still remains. Using the first approach and the emphasis on structural constraints it is possible to argue that this example demonstrates the role of powerful organisations carrying with them incorporated norms that prevent women from entering technical occupations. However, this does not answer the question for which institutions and with which norm gender and working class background can serve as indicators in this example. The second approach stresses the importance of experiences, interpretations and preferences of respondents who had to make a selection from institutionalised options, but fails to provide us with hypotheses about concrete interpretations and preferences actors would develop in certain situations.

Consequently, both approaches have something in common. They represent general orientation hypotheses or a heuristic framework rather than tightly woven theories, and it is almost impossible to deduce from them empirically content-rich hypotheses about concrete norms of concrete institutions or hypotheses about concrete aspirations of concrete actors without further additional assumptions. Taking the above-mentioned example as a case in point, a variety of additional assumptions could be formulated *ad hoc*: it could be assumed that employers and gatekeepers of vocational education and training - led by gender-stereotypical norms - regard certain occupations as inappropriate for females and discourage or prevent young women from applying for certain apprenticeships. One can also think of gender-stereotypical socialisation processes at school which lower young females' interests in technical matters. The problem of inventing such additional assumptions *ad hoc* becomes clear if one takes into account that mere socio-demographic data of the kind presented above can also be used by socio-biologists as confirming evidence for assumed genetic differences between the sexes.

For a better understanding of the methodological and theoretical problems it may also be helpful to refer to the distinction between the "hard core" of a research programme and its "protective belt" made by Imre Lakatos (1982). The leading assumptions of sociological theories (or the "hard core" of sociological research programmes) often do not suffice to derive propositions about concrete empirical facts. The apparent gap between general theoretical assumptions and concepts on the one hand and empirical data on the other has then to be bridged by further empirical, content-rich and auxiliary assumptions. Such "bridge assumptions" (Lindenberg 1992; Kelle and Lüdemann 1995; Kelle and Lüdemann 1997) often play an important role in theory building, particularly in sociology. The function of the hard core remains restricted to a heuristic theory construction which serves as a "skeleton" to which the "flesh" of bridge assumptions is added, thus increasing the empirical content of the resulting theory.

In order to develop bridge assumptions about culture-specific or situation-specific preferences, norms, values or attitudes, social researchers who work with socio-demographic data can often draw on their common sense knowledge. Knowledge about generally accepted norms or about preferences of other members of a given culture usually forms an integral part of culturally or sub-culturally specific stocks of everyday knowledge. However, since a great deal of this knowledge is self-evident or implicit, the heuristic nature of the researcher's common sense knowledge is seldom made explicit. Instead it serves as a shadow methodology of theory construction. In many cases this methodology would cause no major harm, especially if research takes place within the researcher's own culture or sub-culture where s/he has easy access to its common sense knowledge. But the shortcomings and limitations of this shadow methodology can easily be discerned if foreign cultures or unfamiliar domestic subcultures are the object of scientific inquiry. Not being a member of those cultures, researchers do not possess sufficient knowledge to formulate hypotheses about preferences, norms and attitudes in the investigated domain. In these cases the shadow methodology can be most harmful, seducing the researcher into deriving hypotheses from his personal common sense knowledge that would completely fail to account for the norms that play a role in the investigated empirical field.

Our approach towards this problem is the systematic integration of qualitative methods into our research about social structures in the life course. By using methods of open interviewing and ethnographic field research we seek to derive bridge assumptions about the aspirations of actors and the specific norms which are relevant in the investigated social domain.

In our research about the occupational life courses of young adults we follow the following three steps:

With the help of socio-demographic and life event data those variables are identified which represent the most important structural influences on the life course. These variables are regarded as "proxies" for specific "social situations" which we define in terms of the opportunities and constraints that are related to a certain social status.

2. Using previous theoretical and common sense knowledge can easily identify some aspects of the social situation. The social status of a graduate from a German "Gymnasium", for instance, relates to the opportunity to attend a university. Other aspects - especially those that are related to specific occupational cultures - have to be carefully investigated with the help of qualitative methods. We use expert interviews to investigate "objective aspects" of social situations, and semi-structured qualitative interviews with our respondents to discern how they subjectively interpret and perceive the opportunities and constraints of their social situation. These efforts result in what can be called "ethnographies of occupational life worlds".

The third step is also conducted with the help of qualitative interviews: we try to identify how the respondents establish a biographically meaningful relationship with the constraints and opportunities of their situation and how they choose between different institutionalised options. While the focus of the second step is on cultural and institutional norms and how different actors perceive them we concentrate in the third step on personal aspirations and strategies.

ETHNOGRAPHIES OF OCCUPATIONAL LIFE WORLDS

In what follows we will use the ethnography of occupational life worlds to shine some light on our statistical results.

The occupational situation of bank employees is characterised by the existence of highly institutionalised career paths. The organisational culture in banks pays high attention towards career development and achievement. Both men and women are expected to take an active part in launching into certain career paths, and they are encouraged to constantly discuss their plans and their achievements with their seniors who monitor and supervise their progress. Whilst there is little difference between men and women on the lower and medium level of management, senior management seems to have a certain reluctance to promote women above a certain level in the hierarchy. Information about such policies is, of course, difficult to obtain from members of the senior management team. However, it seems that men are more often encouraged to enter a university to study economics or business administration upon completion of their apprenticeship than their female counterparts. Reasons that are given by senior managers for a gender-specific promotion policy almost always include the "risk" of pregnancy and motherhood.

The role of gender-stereotypical promotion strategies is even more pronounced in the field of retail sales. In particular, large grocery and department stores offer highly differentiated career paths with few differences between the level of responsibility and authority at each rung of the career ladder. In this occupation women face a much higher risk than men of remaining at the lower levels of the occupational hierarchy. Consequently, the greater tendency for women to leave this occupation could be explained by lacking career opportunities.

The vocational training in office work equips the apprentice with a broad qualification that allows him to work in almost any administrative field. This occupational range offers high job security and good opportunities to change employers. It is these factors which may explain the high "holding capacity" of this occupation. A further attraction of this vocation, especially for women, is that office work offers various possibilities for part time work which makes it easier to form a family and raise children.

An apprenticeship in car mechanics almost always takes place in small workshops and companies have been accused of using their apprentices as cheap labour. This also means that job security and promotion prospects at the end of the vocational training are limited. Apprentices in the field of hairdressing face similar problems. The qualification as a hairdresser is often associated with bad working conditions and low salaries. This situation can, to a large extent, account for the significant migration out of in these occupations. It is also worth mentioning that a large proportion of female hairdressers would not choose this training voluntarily, had it not been because they didn't find an apprenticeship in another occupation.

Industrial mechanics are in most cases trained in large companies and in the old core industries such as engine building and the automobile industry. The training takes place in special training workshops with highly qualified master craftsmen. The industrial mechanic has always been regarded as one of the most prestigious occupations in this sector - comparable with a working class aristocracy. Following formal training, most of the industrial mechanics have in the past received permanent employment contracts by their companies. However, our sample of industrial mechanics entered the labour market in a period of economic recession which hit the German manufacturing and mechanical engineering industry very hard. Consequently, the work situation upon completion of the apprenticeship became much less privileged than their training would have led them to expect. The majority of newly trained industrial mechanics had to perform tasks that did not differ from the work of unskilled and semi-skilled workers. However, only a minority of industrial mechanics regarded the apprenticeship as their final educational investment. For many, entering higher education was the ultimate goal. Against this background it is important to understand that many employers in Germany are interested in graduates who possess a qualification as both an industrial mechanic (showing the graduate's ability for and knowledge of the practical aspects of machine building) and an engineer (thus demonstrating analytic skills and theoretical knowledge).

THE ROLE OF BIOGRAPHICAL ORIENTATIONS IN THE OCCUPATIONAL LIFE COURSE

Which aspirations and strategies do adolescents and young adults develop when faced with different occupational situations? To answer this question our semi-structured qualitative interviews are analysed with the help of an "axial coding scheme" (Strauss and Corbin 1990; Witzel 1996). This allows us to investigate three main aspects of each step in the occupational career:

1. The aspirations of the respondent,
2. the way the respondent tried to translate their aspirations into actions (realisation of aspirations) and
3. the way the respondent assessed the outcomes of their actions (assessments)

By comparing the respondent's aspirations, realisations and assessments over some years of the life course we find that most individuals develop a characteristic and stable mode of coping with the opportunities and constraints of their occupational situation. We call these modes "biographical action orientations" ("Biographische Gestaltungsmodi") and use a German typology of six of these modes (Witzel 1998; Heinz, Kelle, Witzel and Zinn 1997) to elaborate on the relation of these action orientations to different occupational situations.

Actors with the mode "Chancenoptimierung" (improvement of opportunities) see work as the crucial domain in life, and work hard to develop their competencies and careers. Since they also regard work as a means of self-fulfilment, they heavily oppose any kind of routine work and expect a high degree of variation and alternation of their tasks. Their readiness to work hard and to perform efficiently is accompanied by the expectation to earn a good salary and to be promoted to a responsible position. In order to achieve their goals these actors often try to engage in some form of "institutional handling" since they try to make use of institutions as a means of developing their careers. In an occupational context which is characterised by routine work and restricted career prospects - as in the case of the industrial mechanic - this "Gestaltungs"-mode leads respondents to redirect their life course by studying for higher school level qualifications and, ultimately, to enter university or a higher technical college.

In an occupational situation characterised by highly institutionalised career trajectories - as in the cases of banking or retail sales - often a more passive biographical action orientation can be observed. We term this orientation "Laufbahnfixierung" - a unique German term which refers to promotion according to an institutionalised plan. This does not mean, however, that respondents with this action orientation are idler or more slothful than others. For most of them work is among the most important things in life. However, they are less "individualised" than actors exhibiting the mode of "Chancenoptimierung". Instead of attempting to improve their opportunities and actively use institutions, they try to adapt themselves to the careers schedules developed for them by their employers.

Both, "Chancenoptimierung" and "Laufbahnfixierung" can be regarded as typical middle class modes. In blue-collar occupations characterised by low wages, insecure job prospects and very limited career opportunities we find frequently those biographical action orientations which are characterised by stagnating perspectives. One of these modes, termed "Lohnarbeiterhabitus" (workmen's habit) is a typical male mode found predominantly among car mechanics and industrial mechanics who are unlikely to change their occupation. Respondents with this mode regard good working conditions and good salary as the most crucial things in their work. Their attitudes towards job and career opportunities are very sober and realistic: they do not see work as a means of self-fulfilment but as a way of bread winning. These workers try to develop strategies to avoid job-related exploitation. It thus comes as no surprise that leisure activities play an important role in their lives.

Another mode of coping with occupational situations with restricted career opportunities, termed "Betriebsidentifizierung" (identification with the company), is - at least in our sample - exclusively adopted by females. The crucial variable for these respondents is a good climate at the workplace, comprising good personal relations to colleagues, company management and customers. The company is often regarded as a "second home". The respondents often address the company as "we" or "the family". These individuals are very loyal to their employer and show a great understanding for demanding business interests. In exchange they expect their employers to endow them with a climate of job security and personal care

The two remaining biographical action orientations, "Persönlichkeitsentwicklung" ("Personal autonomy") and "Selbständigenhabitus" ("self-employed habitus") play only a limited role in the occupational fields which were the subjects of our investigation. Personal autonomy emphasises that an occupation should serve individual self-realisation and that work must be meaningful and morally acceptable. Finally, "self-employed habitus" sees work as a means of economic success and individual risk taking in order to maintain entrepreneurial independence.

CONCLUDING REMARKS

Our results demonstrate the long-term influence of the occupation trained for on career developments. The risk of leaving the occupation is highly dependent on the kind of occupation for which individuals were trained. Our analysis shows that whilst banking and office work exhibit a high continuity of occupational status, occupations from technical, industrial or trade domains have a lower "holding capacity". Furthermore, it was possible to identify a specific interaction between gender and occupation trained for, which can be explained through the differences in occupational cultures. Apart from gender specific promotion policies, self-selection also plays an important role. Workers in middle management positions, such as section or branch managers, are usually heavily overburdened with work and are expected to undertake a lot of overtime work. Consequently, many women who plan to have children do not seek careers of this kind, since they anticipate conflicts between different role expectations at home and in the work place.

However, different occupations are not only linked to different career opportunities but also to differences in the risk of job insecurity and short term employment. As a result, occupations in the technical, industrial or trade domain show more discontinuity of the occupational life course.

Our analysis also demonstrates that the system of vocational education and training (VET) in Germany represents a powerful institution which guides, controls and influences the occupational life course of young German adults. As for the intergenerational reproduction of social inequality, our results show a complex picture: we find a measurable influence of gender and social origin on the access to training in a particular occupation. Young people with a middle class background have greater chances to access training in occupations with promising career prospects and low risks of occupational instability, while those individuals with a working class background are more likely to be trained in occupations with restricted occupational outlooks. However, the influence of social class background is mediated through the German three-tier school system which also diminishes and mitigates the influences of properties such as class origin and gender, by allowing competence and motivation to have an influence on school attainment.

The influence of social class origin, which is of considerable importance for the level of school qualification attainment, and thus influences the transition into the occupational life course, is further weakened during the first years of working life. Actors have to permanently make active efforts to preserve their resource endowments. Biographical action orientations thus have an important role to play when it comes to the explanation of variations between occupational careers. Under certain circumstances actors may find ways to cope well with the constraints of an unfavourable economic situation and to open up new career perspectives. Certainly, such processes of reorientation are supported by the German system of VET, since this system helps endow the apprentices of certain occupations with broad qualifications that can be transferred to other occupational areas. By allowing young people to acquire certificates and qualifications, the Dual System ensures flexibility and transparency while lowering information costs: employers can easily find workers with specific key-qualifications. German VET is thus capable of smoothing the path from school to work and work to work.

REFERENCES

Blossfeld, H. P. (1993), "Changes in Educational Opportunities in the Federal Republic of Germany. A Longitudinal Study of Cohorts Born between 1916 and 1965", in: Shavit, Y. and Blossfeld, H. P. (eds.): *Persistent Inequality: Changing Educational Stratification in Thirteen Countries.* Boulder, Colorado, pp. 51-74.

Blossfeld, H. P. and Shavit, Y. (1993), Persisting barrierrs: Changes in Educational Opportunities in Thirteen Countries, in Shavit, Y. and Blossfeld, H. P. (eds.): *Persistent Inequality: Changing Educational Stratification in Thirteen Countries.* Boulder, Co: Westview, pp. 1-24.

Creswell, J. W. (1994), *Research Design. Qualitative and Quantitative Approaches.* Thousands Oaks: Sage.

Denzin, N. (1977), *The Research Act. A Theoretical Introduction to Sociological Methods*, New York: McGraw Hill.

Fielding, N.G. and Fielding, J. L. (1986), *Linking Data. Qualitative Research Methods*, Volume 4, Beverly Hills: Sage.

Flick, U. (1992), "Triangulation Revisited: Strategy of Validation or Alternative", *Journal for the Theory of Social Behaviour*, vol. 22, no.2, pp. 175-197.

Heinz, W. R. (1992), "Introduction: Institutional Gatekeeping and Biographical Agency", in Heinz, W. R. (ed.): *Institutions and Gatekeeping in the Life Course.* Weinheim: Deutscher Studienverlag, pp. 9-30.

Heinz, W. R. (1996a), "Youth transitions in Cross-Cultural Perspective: School-to-Work in Germany", in Galaway, B. and Hudson, J. (eds.), *Youth in Transition. Perspectives on Research and Policy*, Toronto: Thompson Educational Publishing.

Heinz, W. R. (1996b), "Job Entry Patterns in Germany: Does the Apprenticeship still deliver?", paper presented at the conference "*New Passages between Education and Employment*", University of Toronto, April.

Heinz, W. R., Kelle, U. Witzel, A and Zinn, J.(1997), "Vocational Training and Career Development in Germany - Results from a Longitudinal Study", forthcoming in *International Journal of Behavioral Development* (1998).

Kelle, U. and Lüdemann, C. (1995), "'Grau, teurer Freund, ist alle Theorie ...': Rational Choice und das Problem der Brückenannahmen, *Kölner Zeitschrift für Soziologie*, vol. 47, no.2, pp. 249-267.

Kelle, U. and Lüdemann, C. (1998), "Does the Concept of Bridge Assumptions Bring us Closer to a Nomothetic Social Science?" in Blossfeld, H. P. and Prein, G. (eds.):

Causation, Actors and Empirical Analysis of Social Processes, Bolder, Co.: Westview.

Krueger, H. (1996), "Normative Interpretations of Biographical Processes" in Weymann, A. and Heinz, W. R. (eds.), *Society and Biography. Interrelationsships between Social Structure, Institutions and the Life Course*, Weinheim: DSV; pp.129-146.

Lakatos, I. (1982), *The Methodology of Scientific Research Programmes. Philosophical Papers, Vol. I.* Cambridge: University of Cambridge Press.

Lindenberg, S. (1992), "The Method of Decreasing Abstraction", in Coleman, J. S. and Fararo, T. J. (eds.), *Rational Choice Theory. Advocacy and Critique*, Newbury Park: Sage, pp. 3 - 20.

Mariak, V. with Kluge, S. (1997), *Die Konstruktion des ordentlichen Menschen. Arbeitsmoral und Normalität im Alltag beruflicher Ausbildung: Standpunkte und Handlungsmuster von Berufserzieherinnen*, Bremen.

Strauss, A. and Corbin, J. (1990), *Basics of Qualitative Research. Grounded Theory Procedures and Techniques*, Newbury Park: Sage.

Witzel, A. (1996), "Auswertung problemzentrierter Interviews. Grundlagen und Erfahrungen" in Strobl, R. and Böttger, A. (eds.), *Wahre Geschichten? Zur Theorie und Praxis qualitativer Interviews*, Baden Baden: Nomos, pp. 49-76.

Witzel, A. and Kühn, T. (1998), *Berufsbiographische Gestaltungsmodi*, mimeo.

Witzel, A., Helling, V. and Mönnich, I. (1996), "Die Statuspassage in den Beruf als Prozeß der Reproduktion sozialer Ungleichheit", in Bolder, A., Heinz, W. R. and Rodax, K. (eds.), *Die Wiederentdeckung der Ungleichheit. Tendenzen in Bildung und Arbeit*, Opladen: Leske.

CHAPTER 7

CAREER AND WAGE DIFFERENCES BETWEEN FEMALE AND MALE ENGINEERS AND SCIENTISTS[13]: THE NORWEGIAN EXPERIENCE

CLARA AASE ARNESEN AND JANE BAEKKEN

INTRODUCTION

Gender equality has been an explicit political goal in Norway for several years. An important strategy has been to encourage women to make non-traditional educational choices. Among others, the purpose has been to strengthen women's opportunities to compete on the same level as men for the most attractive jobs, in terms of both wages and prestige. A major objective has been the levelling of differences in the labour market as a result of female-oriented education. It is argued that the latter leads all too often to employment in the public sector and is among the factors that cause Norwegian women to have lower wages than men. By encouraging women to choose an education that qualifies for occupations in the private sector, it is believed that a broader female representation and an increase in the percentage proportion of women in higher positions can be achieved.

When women enter a typical male education, however, some doubts remain as to whether this is *sufficient* to secure a more even distribution of material and social returns to work. This chapter will take a closer look at both the career paths and wage developments of two cohorts of scientists and graduate engineers. We will study indicators of women's achievements in the labour market compared to those of men during the first few years of work. We will examine employment in the private sector and promotion to leading positions and analyse whether differences between men and women can be explained by individual factors such as work activity rates and work preferences. We also assess the extent to which wage differences between male and female scientists and graduate engineers are due to differences in human capital,

---

[13] In this paper the term "scientist" refers to graduates in natural sciences.

different distributions by college majors and types of jobs. Finally, we aim to highlight the extent to which these differences are caused by discrimination in the Norwegian labour market.

THE THEORY

In general, male-dominated occupations have better promotion opportunities than female-dominated occupations. This is partly caused by behavioural patterns among women and men in the labour market, and partly by characteristics of the labour market itself. Establishments employing mainly women are less likely to have developed internal labour markets than establishments employing mainly men (Baron, Davis-Blake and Bielby 1986). Furthermore, it has been argued that leading positions are valued more in male than in female-dominated professions and organisations (Rasmussen 1994). It is also worth pointing out that in many male occupations, an investment in career-related factors, including longer working hours, additional education and on-the-job training is assumed to be more rewarding than seniority considerations (Hoel 1995). As a consequence and in line with the theory of human capital (Becker 1981) women who give priority to a career over and above child rearing will be more inclined to choose a male-oriented education and field of occupation than women who attribute greater importance to their family. Once a male occupation has been chosen, it is unlikely that career plans will change dramatically. The decision to opt for a male occupation becomes a self-feeding mechanism: it is male occupations that are associated with high opportunity costs (loss of income, career delays, etc.) and rational behaviour prevents frequent interruptions or reduced working hours.

More recent theories, however, allow for nuances to this picture, and suggest that occupational choices are of a relatively short-term nature, partly because of work uncertainties (Jacobs 1990). Male professions adjusted to a typical male career pattern may steer women to areas of work where family and work can be combined, and where there is less financial punishment associated with career interruptions. This explains why the percentage proportion of women employed in the public sector is higher than that of men. In general, the public sector in Norway offers higher job security, but weaker wage and career prospects than the private sector.

It has been claimed, and over time well documented, that women have other preferences and attitudes towards work than men. Research on graduate engineering students, for instance, has shown that while male students were preoccupied with such features as high wages and status in their future careers, for women socially beneficial work and a good work environment were valued higher than factors related to wages and prestige (Kvande and Rasmussen 1990). Thus, differences in occupational preferences may contribute to explaining possible differences between the percentage proportion of men and women employed in the private sector. Several studies have also shown that women and men select their areas of study very differently, with women usually opting for areas with a lower rate of monetary return (Polachek 1978). In addition to activity rates, family situation and occupational preferences, the area of academic study will thus be included in our analysis of the probability of being employed in the private sector.

The literature on promotion opportunities in male-dominated occupations indicates that it is possible for women to be promoted to leading positions. The probability of achieving such positions depends, however, on a number of crucial factors, including stability in the labour market, additional investment in professional development and occupational standing. Withdrawal from the labour market due to family obligations may have a negative effect on promotion possibilities. Women who work in the public sector may to a greater extent have achieved leading positions than women who work in private sector companies. There is reason to believe that political goals of gender equality experience less resistance (Ellingsaeter and Rubery 1997), and that relatively more weight is put on seniority status in the public than in the private sector. We will examine the impact of such variables as labour market stability, further education and employment by industrial classification on the probability of women and men to be promoted to a leading position.

Most of the empirical analyses of wage differences between males and females are based on human capital theory. This theory was developed in the 1960's and 1970's on the basis that there is a close positive relationship between a person's human capital, productivity and the rate of pay (Schultz 1961; Becker 1964; Mincer 1974). Education and work experience serve as main indicators of human capital and are included in almost all empirical analyses of wage differences. Women's generally lower level of education and shorter periods of work experience have thus been held responsible for their lower wages compared to those of their male counterparts.

However, several analyses of male and female rates of pay show that differences in education and work experience explain only a small proportion of the wage differential. A Norwegian analysis (Barth 1992) found that human capital factors reduce the wage gap by only four percent. The small proportion of the wage differential between males and females accounted for by human capital factors has led to a discussion about how to measure a person's human capital. Analyses on how to improve the modelling of wage differentials during the first few years of a person's career suggest that "total work experience" may need to be replaced by an indicator that takes the type and frequency of work into account (continuous work, full-time or part-time work, etc.) (Light and Ureta 1995). Periods without paid work result in a depreciation of human capital, at least in the short run, and can reduce wage rates (Mincer and Ofek 1982). Part-time work is expected to have a negative impact on wages because employers perceive the part-time character of employment as a negative signal. As a consequence, employers are less willing to invest in on-the-job training for part-time workers (Gullason 1990). Those working part-time may also feel a weaker attachment to the labour market and may be less interested in on-the-job training. As women generally work more part-time and are more likely to experience a discontinued labour market pattern than men, it comes as no surprise that women receive lower wages than men. Even when this is taken into account, however, human capital factors fail to explain a substantial proportion of the wage gap between men and women.

The small proportion of the wage differential between males and females accounted for by human capital factors has also led to a discussion on whether other productivity-related factors should be included in analyses of wage differences. Some analyses include variables such as job preferences, type of education and more detailed employment characteristics. It has also been argued that total compensation for a job needs to be sub-divided into pecuniary and non-pecuniary factors, and that non-pecuniary factors ought to be included in analyses of wage differences for highly educated individuals (Mathios 1989). The importance attached to pecuniary and non-pecuniary compensation depends on a person's preferences and priorities. As mentioned earlier, men and women appear to have different job preferences. Empirical studies have shown that those who place a high level of importance on traditional male objectives such as "being a leader" or "making a lot of money" were rewarded with better prospects for promotion, whereas those who place a high level of importance on traditional female objectives were not (Daymont and Andrisani 1984). Different personal preferences and priorities thus also contribute to the explanation of wage differences between male and female workers.

Other empirical investigations have shown that an education's gender composition influences wages. A male-oriented education tends to result in higher wages (Polachek 1978; Rumberger and Thomas 1993). The type of job is also an important factor in explaining wage differences in general. The wage gap between males and females is reduced when characteristics of the job are included in the analysis. There is a tendency for women to be channelled into jobs with lower wages compared to those held by men (Wood, Corcoran and Courant 1993; Barth 1992). Women in male-dominated occupations hold, on average, positions with lower rates of pay than similar positions of their male colleagues (Kvande and Rasmussen 1990; Reskin and Roos 1990).

The inclusion of personal preferences and job characteristics in analyses of wage differences between males and females is controversial, particularly if the main purpose of the analysis is to focus on discrimination. The reason is that the variables themselves can be affected by discrimination (Cain 1986). However, as one of our main purposes is to understand what leads to wage differences between men and women, we will include job preferences and job characteristics at least in some parts of our analysis.

We expect all these factors to explain some of the wage gap between male and female scientists and graduate engineers. Although female scientists and graduate engineers have a much stronger labour market attachment than female workers in general, we expect that differences in human capital factors account for some of the wage gap. We also expect, however, that job characteristics will explain a substantial part of the wage differential between male and female scientists and graduate engineers.

EMPIRICAL RESULTS

The following analysis of career and wage differences between male and female scientists and engineers is based on a survey carried out in 1994 by the Norwegian Institute for Studies in Research and Higher Education. The survey examines two cohorts of graduates (1985/86 and 1989/90, respectively, i.e. our study concentrates on graduates who are relatively early in their careers). The survey includes the complete work history and current labour market situation, the extent of non-employment and temporary leaves, family situation, occupational values and earnings. We first present results of the analysis of career developments followed by results of the analysis of wage differentials.

Employment in the private sector

In both cohorts the percentage proportion of women working in the private sector at the time of the survey was relatively high, but lower than that of men. In the 1985/86 cohort, 65 per cent of women and 74 per cent of men worked in the private sector. In the 1989/90 cohort, the corresponding figures were 48 per cent and 65 per cent, respectively. In what follows we analyse the impact of working activity, caring for children and occupational preferences on the probability of working in the private sector. In order to study as to whether these factors have different effects on men and women we have carried out separate analyses. The technique used is a logistic regression. The explanatory variables are largely dichotomous to simplify the interpretation of results. The model assumes a non-linear relationship between the probability of working in the private sector and the independent variables, with the probability varying between 0 and 1.

If male occupations, especially in the private sector, demand high work activity rates, we assume that this has an isolated positive impact on the probability of working in the private sector. This could reduce women's probability of employment in the private sector more than men's, since relatively more women experience some temporary leave from the labour market, mainly in the form of paid parental leave. Work activity is measured by "number of person-months". For each cohort we estimate the average number of person-months (with leaves and non-employment deducted) and introduce a categorical variable, where the number of person-months above average is given the value 1 and 0 otherwise. Furthermore, we assume that reduced working hours occur mainly in the public sector, and that scientists and graduate engineers who have previously worked part-time have a higher probability of working in the public sector. A respondent who has worked part-time is given the value 1, and 0 otherwise[14].

"Number of children" is another important variable. Childcare responsibilities may increase the difficulties of having a demanding job. In the analysis we thus include a continuos variable for the number of children. More female scientists than graduate engineers appear to have children in the transition to the labour market. This can be

---

[14] This is somewhat problematic, since "having worked part-time" may include respondents who have had insignificant periods of part-time work.

explained by the fact that scientists were on average older than graduate engineers. However, our data also show that female graduate engineers seem to have their first child at a later stage in their career compared with data of female scientists. To take account of these differences, we include an interaction variable for children and educational background.

Even though female scientists and graduate engineers have chosen a non-traditional education, they are over-represented in some areas of academic study. It is possible that those areas of study with a relatively high percentage proportion of women are steered towards the public sector, and that "area of study" has an isolated impact on sector employment. We include a variable which indicates whether or not the respondent graduated from a "gender-neutral" area of study.

To capture the influence of different attitudes to work, we include occupational preferences[15] in our analysis. The variables for occupational values are dichotomised, where those with a factor value of 0.4 or higher are given the value 1, and 0 otherwise. However, the inclusion of occupational preferences is problematic since the relationship between the occupation of an individual and occupational preference is ambiguous. Do occupational preferences affect the type of job chosen, or does the chosen type of job influence an individual's occupational preference? We defend our approach by reference to numerous comparisons between preferences among youth, students and employees that point to stability in occupational values.

Traditionally, graduate engineers have a stronger attachment to the private sector than scientists. In addition, the transition to the private sector after completed education is weaker for cohorts educated in the late 1980's. The poor labour market in the private sector may be an explanation for this observation. Control variables for the effects of both educational background and different cohorts are included. The base category refers to graduate engineers in the 1985/86 cohort. The results of our separate analyses of males and females are shown in Table 1. The sign of the coefficient can be interpreted as an increasing (positive) or decreasing (negative) probability of being employed in the private sector.

Our separate analyses give us some interesting insights into gender-specific employability patterns. For example, the number of person-months has an impact mainly on men's employment in the private sector. This may be because men and women have different types of jobs. Furthermore, our results show that there is a negative, but non-significant relationship between having worked part-time and work in the private sector. Graduating from areas of academic study with a relatively high female representation has a negative impact only on males' probability of working in the private sector. The

---

[15] Through factor analysis, a set of 23 variables on job conditions was reduced to 5 factors or preferences. They are: "professional preferences", including attitudes towards a academic/scientific career ; "company preferences", including conditions such as concerns about adding value to the company; "leadership preferences", including the achievement of high wages and leading positions; "social preferences", including attitudes towards the work's meaning for society; and finally "security preferences", including factors such as work pressures, living conditions in the area of work, etc.

number of children does not reduce the probability for women to be employed in the private sector. However, when controlled for educational background we find that having children has a significant negative impact for female scientists. That this is not the case for female graduate engineers could be partly due to the differences in timing of the birth of the first child. Since graduate engineers are employed largely in the private sector, it is also possible that women have other types of jobs in the private sector than men and that they find "niches" in the labour market where, until recently, it has been uncommon to combine childcare with gainful employment.

Table 1:   Logistic regression of the probability of working in the private sector. Graduate engineers and scientists, 1985/86 and 1989/90 cohorts.

	Men		Women	
	Coeff.	Relative risk[c]	Coeff.	Relative risk
Constant	1.43[a]		1.26[a]	
Scientist 1985/86	-1.05[a]	0.35	-0.32	0.73
Graduate engineer 1989/90	-0.38[a]	0.69	-0.75[a]	0.47
Scientist 1989/90	-1.47[a]	0.23	-1.55[a]	0.21
"Gender-neutral" field of study	-0.24[b]	0.78	0.03	1.03
Work activity	0.27[b]	1.31	-0.17	0.84
Working hours (part-time)	-0.35	0.71	-0.19	0.83
Children	-0.11	0.90	-0.05	0.95
Scientist*children	0.10	1.11	-0.54[b]	0.59
Professional preferences	-0.31[a]	0.74	0.09	1.10
Company preferences	0.63[a]	1.88	0.64[a]	1.89
Leadership preferences	0.82[a]	2.26	0.00	1.00
Social preferences	-0.83[a]	0.44	-1.34[a]	0.26
Security preferences	0.39[a]	1.48	0.13	1.14
Number of observations	1 173		415	

a) Significant at the 0.05 level,
b) Significant at the 0.10 level
c) Relative risk (odds) is estimated from the coefficient, which is the logarithm to the odds. The isolated effect of an independent variable is converted into exp(coeff.). For example, the relative risk, or odds, for a male scientist in the 1985/86 cohort of working in the private sector is exp (-1.05) = 0.35.

Our analysis also indicates that both "leadership preferences" and "company preferences" increase the employment probability of male scientists and graduate engineers in the private sector. For females, however, "leadership preferences" have no significant impact on the probability of private sector employment. Thus, women with preferences towards leading positions have no higher probability of working in the private sector than women without such preferences. Furthermore, the positive effect of "company preferences" on the probability of being employed in the private sector appears to be equally strong for men and women. As for "job security preferences" our analysis is unable to identify a significant impact on women's employment in the private sector. Both female scientists and female graduate engineers seem to put great emphasis on such values, yet it does not seem to be the case that women with strong preferences towards job security are more inclined to work in the public sector.

All in all, we identify several factors that reduce the employment probability of women with a male-oriented education in the private sector. Because of requirements for high work activity rates in the private sector, women, in their role as provider of domestic childcare, are more likely to be employed in the public sector than their male counterparts. There are also indications that women's choices of academic study may reduce possibilities of employment in the private sector. Although these findings are revealing they fail to provide sufficient empirical evidence in support of lower employment probabilities in the private sector for women than for men.

Leading positions

We now turn to the examination of the effect of human capital and occupational standing on the probability of having been promoted to a leading position. The percentage proportion of respondents in leading positions at the time of the survey amounted to 26 per cent among males and 17 per cent among females[16]. The female share of leading occupational positions within companies is lower than that of men, both in the public and private sector. However, the difference is particularly pronounced in the private sector.

We expect both labour market participation and occupational standing to impact on the possibilities for promotion to a leading position. However, a number of other variables will also need to be taken into account. For example, there is reason to believe that caring for very young children is particularly difficult to combine with a leading occupational position, and we include a variable for those individuals who have children aged 7 years or younger. Furthermore, we include a variable for those who graduated from a "gender-neutral" area of academic study to investigate whether women's choices of specific areas of academic study are of any statistical significance.

Standard industrial classifications facilitate our analysis. The reference category includes economic activities which take place mainly in the public sector: public services (public administration and schools), universities, colleges and scientific institutes. Other categories include the oil sector, other manufacturing industries and private services. The final category includes mainly technical services, business services and communication,

---

[16] The respondents stated the percentage proportion of time spent on work tasks, and "leading position" is defined on the basis of the most time-consuming task. Those who spent 30 per cent or more of their working time on administration and leadership, or stated this as the task they spent most time on, have been classified as being in a leading position.

together with a small number of retail trade and financial services. Control variables that distinguish different cohorts and types of education are also included.

Table 2: **Logistic regression of the probability of working in a leading position. Graduate engineers and natural scientists, 1985/86 and 1989/90 cohorts.**

	Men		Women	
	Coeff.	Rel. risk	Coeff.	Rel. risk
Constant	-2.18[a]		-1.58[a]	
Graduate engineer	0.53[a]	1.69	0.87[a]	2.39
89/90 cohorts	-0.64[a]	0.53	-0.96[a]	0.38
Work activity (above average)	0.43[a]	1.53	0.16	1.17
Working hours (part-time)	-0.38	0.68	-0.07	0.93
"Gender-neutral" field of study	-0.30[b]	0.74	-0.26	0.77
Further education (bus./adm., law)	0.81[a]	2.24	0.91[b]	2.49
Children 7-years-old or younger	0.06	1.06	-0.56	0.57
Oil sector	0.52[a]	1.68	0.20	1.22
Other manufacturing industry	1.05[a]	2.87	0.13	1.14
Private services	0.96[a]	2.60	0.05	1.05
Number of observations	1 194		430	

a Significant at the 0.05 level
b Significant at the 0.10 level

Our analysis demonstrates that graduate engineers have a higher probability of being in a leading position than scientists, with the 1985/86 cohort having a higher probability of being in a leading position than the 1989/90 cohort. Having worked more than average numbers of person-months increases the probability of being in a leading position for men, while there is no isolated effect of work activity for women. This might be because at the time of the survey relatively more women were in leading positions in the public sector, where seniority is assumed to be as significant for promotion as work activity.

Graduating from areas of academic study with a relatively high female representation reduces the probability of a leading position for a male graduate engineer or scientist. Further education in subjects that can be related to leadership aspirations increases the probability of being in a leading position for both males and females. In fact, the odds of being in a leading position more than doubled if the respondent had taken or was undertaking this type of further education. Although the presence of young children in a respondent's household reduces the probability of being in leading occupational positions for women, it is interesting to note that this result is statistically insignificant. Working under the assumption that a combination of leading occupational positions and family obligations is more acceptable in the public than in the private sector, the fact that women achieve leading positions in both sectors may reduce a possible negative impact of children on promotion possibilities in the private sector.

The probability of having been promoted to a leading position by industrial group shows clearly that female graduate engineers and scientists have different recruitment patterns than their male contemporaries. The analysis of male graduate engineers and scientists shows that compared to employment in public services being employed in the manufacturing industry increases the odds of being in a leading position by nearly three times. Employment in private services also increases the probability of a leading position considerably. The effect for those employed in the oil sector, albeit somewhat weaker, points in the same direction.

These results are not surprising *per se*. Graduate engineers and natural scientists are recruited to leading positions in their traditional occupational areas. What is interesting to observe, however, is that while this is the case for males, we do not find the same evidence for females. In our analysis of women, none of the other industrial groups increase the probability of a leading position relative to employment in public services. The results of our analysis do, however, indicate that female graduate engineers and scientists have a more even distribution of leading positions than their male counterparts. In comparison, a larger percentage proportion of men is in a leading occupational position that is associated with high wages and occupational status.

Wages

Our strategy for analysing the wage differential between male and female scientists and graduate engineers is first to perform a regression analysis of the natural logarithm of gross wages[17] in 1994 on

- human capital
- preferences or occupational values and
- type of education and job.

As measures of human capital, we use the following variables: additional higher education, academic grades, years of labour market participation after graduation, months out of the labour market and months in part-time work[18]. Our second explanatory variable, occupational preferences, is measured by the following: professional, company, leadership, social and security preferences. Finally, our third explanatory feature, type of education and work, is measured by distinguishing between scientist and graduate engineer status, cohort, graduation from a "gender-neutral" or male dominated education, sector of employment (private/public) and industrial classification. We also include indicators for the geographical location of the workplace and take into account whether

---

[17] As a measure of wages we use gross, ordinary monthly rates of pay. Pay for over-time, bonuses and extra job rewards are excluded as is the examination of self-employed individuals.

[18] We define part-time work as less than 80 per cent of hours worked full-time.

the person is a PhD student[19] and whether the person held a leading occupational position.

Table 3. Variable Means - Men and women. N=1190

	Men	Women
Number of observations	924	267
Log (wages)	10.079	9.998
Additional education (per cent)	0.264	0.255
Grades (per cent above the median)	0.563	0.439
Work experience (years)	6.101	5.880
(Work experience)^2	41.979	38.509
Non-employment (months)	1.555	7.303
Part time (months)	0.487	2.772
Professional preferences	0.047	-0.044
Company preferences	0.008	0.036
Leadership preferences	0.064	-0.256
Society preferences	-0.039	0.112
Security preferences	-0.073	0.211
Graduate engineer (per cent)	0.719	0.608
Graduate engineer 1989/90-cohort (per cent)	0.384	0.392
"Gender-neutral" education (per cent)	0.190	0.460
Leading position (per cent)	0.221	0.147
Research recruitment job (per cent)	0.060	0.117
Industry 1. Primary, secondary industry ,excl. oil sector (per cent)	0.213	0.171
Industry 2. Oil sector (per cent)	0.116	0.13
Industry 3. Retail and communications industry (per cent)	0.054	0.061
Industry 4. Finance and business services (per cent)	0.268	0.165
Industry 5. Community, social and personal services (per cent)	0.347	0.459
Sector (per cent in private sector)	0.689	0.565
Geographical location of workplace (per cent in big cities)	0.792	0.834

Descriptive data on the key variables used in the analyses are shown in Table 3. The results indicate that the wage gap between male and female scientists and graduate engineers amounts to about 8 per cent. Female scientists and graduate engineers show a very strong attachment to the labour market during the first years after graduation, although there are some differences between men and women. Table 3 shows that women spend more time in non-employment and work on average a little more part-time

---

[19] Norwegian PhD students are, in fact, wage earners, i.e. their grants are given in terms of a wage. Though they may start out with a salary comparable to those of their cohort who go into civil jobs, their wages stay approximately the same throuhout thir work on the dissertation while other graduates profit from promotions and wage increases.

than their male colleagues. Table 3 also shows that male and female scientists and graduate engineers pursue different majors and that they to some extent hold different types of jobs. As mentioned previously, males are more inclined to hold jobs associated with high earnings.

Finally, Table 4 shows the result of the regression analysis as facilitated by three different models. Model 1 shows the results when only human capital factors are included. Model 2 incorporates occupational values and preferences together with human capital variables while Model 3 includes type of education and job together with human capital. Occupational preferences are not included in Model 3 because of the strong correlation between occupational preferences and the chosen type of education and job, respectively.

In Model 1 the most striking result is that non-employment and part-time work have a significant negative impact on the wages of male (but not female) scientists and graduate engineers. As for other human capital variables, no major differences between men and women occur. Model 2 shows that men who placed particular emphasis on being in a leading position and making a lot of money have somewhat higher wages compared to women who did the same. Social preferences seem to have a negative influence on wages for both men and women, although the impact is strongest for females. Finally, Model 3 shows that the inclusion of "type of education and job" has a major impact on wages of both male and female scientists and graduate engineers. The most striking differences between males and females are the differences in pay for graduate engineers from the 1989/90 cohort and for PhD students. The large wage difference between male and female scientists and graduate engineers who study towards a PhD is due to the higher percentage proportion of women in the 1985/86 cohort. Women appear to study longer for a PhD than men.

It is, however, interesting to note that while men who perceived being a leader as important received higher wages than corresponding women (model 2), no wage differences can be observed between men and women who have actually taken up a leading position (model 3). One explanation for this result is that men and women pursue careers in different labour markets. A higher proportion of female scientists and graduate engineers had careers in the lower-paying public sector than their male counterparts. Another explanation is that female scientists and graduate engineers with leader preferences use more time to obtain a leading position than their male colleagues because of childbirth/care obligations. A final explanation could be that employers discriminate against women in the recruitment process for leading positions. This assertion is supported by an analysis of graduate engineers in six Norwegian companies which found that fewer women were offered leading positions than men although many of the women were interested in such positions (Kvande and Rasmussen 1990).

Table 4. Regression of log wages. N (men)=924 and N (women)=267.

	Model 1		Model 2		Model 3	
	Men	Women	Men	Women	Men	Women
Constant	9.768^a	9.678^a	9.751^a	9.592^a	9.624^a	9.612^a
Additional education	0.015	-0.019	0.021^b	0.003	0.044^a	0.022
Grades	0.010	0.019	0.024^a	0.024	0.032^a	0.035^a
Work experience	0.0642^a	0.0631	0.0678^a	0.1034^b	0.0495^a	0.059
(Work experience)^2	-0.0019	-0.0016	-0.0024	-0.0051	-0.0017	-0.0034
Non-employment	-0.006^a	0.001	-0.0045^a	0.000	-0.0035^a	0.0001
Part-time	-0.004^a	0.000	-0.002	0.000	-0.0003	0.000
Professional preferences			-0.016^a	-0.022^a		
Company preferences			0.039^a	0.039^a		
Leadership preferences			0.047^a	0.028^a		
Society preferences			-0.020^a	-0.058^a		
Security preferences			-0.022^a	-0.025^a		
Graduate engineer					0.037^a	0.051^a
Graduate eng.1989/90					-0.033^b	-0.091^a
"Gender-neutral" education					0.010	-0.008
Leading position					0.065^a	0.060^a
PhD student					-0.086^a	-0.139^a
Industry 1					0.054^a	0.093^a
Industry 2					0.154^a	0.156^a
Industry 3					0.084^a	0.037
Industry 4					0.099^a	0.060^a
Sector					0.143^a	0.136^a
Geographical location					0.019	0.046^a
R^2 adjusted	22.9	20.8	34.6	38.8	55.4	71.1

a   Significant at the 0.05 level
b   Significant at the 0.10 level

DISCUSSION

Our analysis shows that male and female scientists and graduate engineers develop their careers differently, with some considerable impact on their wages. Wages of male scientists and graduate engineers are on average about 8 per cent higher compared to those of female colleagues. Some of the differences in career development can be traced back to different family responsibilities. The upbringing of children causes women to have a slower career development than men. Women have to compete in a labour market that seems to be designed for a typical male career path. This has led some women to choose jobs other than those traditionally held by scientists and graduate engineers, i.e. jobs with a lower wage level. The analysis has also shown that females seem to experience some delay in being promoted to leading occupational positions. Furthermore, these promotions seem to come too late to level wage differences. Other research (Barth and Yin 1994) has shown that promotions early in a career are more significant for wage development. Thus, even though women may have a male-dominated education, their lifetime income will be lower than that of men. Despite this criticism, however, it is important to realise that although female scientists and graduate engineers receive somewhat lower wages than their male counterparts, they earn more than they would have done if they had chosen a female-oriented education. Against this background, encouraging women to choose a "male-oriented education" appears to be a successful strategy to move towards gender equality in the Norwegian labour market.

REFERENCES

Baron, J.N., A. Davis-Blake and W.T. Bielby (1986), "The Structure of Opportunity: How Promotion Ladders Vary within and among Organizations", *Administrative Science Quarterly*, vol. 31, pp. 248-273.

Barth, E. (1992), *Loennsforskjeller mellom kvinner og menn i Norge*, Oslo, Institute for Social Research, Report 92:7.

Barth, E. and H. Yin (1994), "Karriere og loennsforskjeller mellom kvinner og menn i departementene, *Soekelys paa arbeidsmarkedet*, vol. 11, 141-145

Becker, G. (1964), *Human Capital*, New York, National Bureau of Economic Research.

Becker, G. (1981), *A Treatise on the Family*, Cambridge, Mass., Harvard University Press.

Cain, G.G. (1986), "The Economic Analysis of Labor Market Discrimination: A Survey" in O. Ashenfelter and R. Layard (eds), *Handbook of Labor Economics*, Amsterdam New York, Oxford, Tokyo, North Holland.

Daymont, T.N. and P.J. Andrisani (1984), "Job Preferences, College Major, and the Gender Gap in Earnings", *The Journal of Human Resources*, XIX no. 3, pp. 408-428.

Ellingsaeter, A.L. and Rubery, J. (1997), "Gender Relations and the Norwegian Labour Market Model", in Doelvik, J.E. and A.H. Steen (eds), *Making Solidarity Work? The*

Norwegian Labour Market Model in Transition, Oslo, Scandinavian University Press.

Gullason, E.T. (1990), "The Effects of Full-Time Versus Part-Time Work Experience on Earnings in "High" and "Low Atrophy" Jobs", *Economics of Education Review*, vol. 9, no. 3, pp. 229-239.

Hoel, M. (1995), *Yrkestilpasning og yrkesutvikling. En studie av arbeidstilknytning, yrkeskarrierer og yrkesmotiver blant et kull hoegskoleutdannede*, Oslo, Institute for Social Research, 1995.

Jacobs, J. (1990), *Revolving Doors. Sex Segregation and Women's Careers*, Stanford, Stanford University Press.

Kvande, E. and B. Rasmussen (1990), *Nye kvinneliv. Kvinner i menns organisasjoner*, Oslo, Ad Notam.

Light A. and M. Ureta (1995), "Early-Career Work Experience and Gender Wage Differentials", *Journal of Labor Economics*, vol. 13, no. 1, pp.121-154.

Mathios, A.D. (1989), Education, Variation in Earnings, and Nonmonetary Compensation, *The Journal of Human Resources*, vol. XXIV, no 3, pp. 456-468.

Mincer, J. (1974), *Schooling, Experience, and Earnings*, New York , National Bureau of Economic Research.

Mincer, J. and H. Ofek (1982), Interrupted Work Careers: Depreciation and Restoration of Human Capital, *The Journal of Human Resources*, vol. XVII, no. 1, pp. 3-24.

Polachek, S.W. (1978), Sex Differences in College Major, *Industrial Labor Review*, vol. 31, no. 4, pp. 498-508.

Rasmussen, B. (1994), Kvinner og ledelse i arbeidslivet: 90-aarenes utfordring. *Soekelys paa arbeidsmarkedet*, vol. 11, pp. 23-27.

Reskin, B.F and P.A. Roos (1990), *Job Queues, Gender Queues*, Philadelphia, Temple University Press.

Rumberger, R.W. and S.L. Thomas (1993), "The Economic Return to College Major, Quality and Performance: A Multilevel Analysis of Recent Graduates", *Economics of Education Review*, vol. 12, no. 12, pp. 1-19.

Schultz, T.W. (1961), "Investment in Human Capital", *American Economic Review*, vol. 51, pp. 1-17.

Wood, R. G., M. E. Corcoran and P. N. Courant (1993), "Pay Differences among the Highly Paid: The Male-Female Earnings Gap in Lawyers' Salaries", *Journal of Labor Economics*, vol. 11, no. 3, pp. 417-441.

PART III

UNEMPLOYMENT AND SOCIAL EXCLUSION

CHAPTER 8

THE EFFECTS OF UNEMPLOYMENT AND MISMATCHES ON FUTURE JOB MATCH AND EARNINGS

A.S.R. VAN DER LINDEN AND R.K.W. VAN DER VELDEN

INTRODUCTION

During the 1980s and 1990s, unemployment among university graduates increased in most European countries. There was also a considerable increase in the number of graduates with jobs below their level of education or jobs that did not match the type of education taken. This increase was due to the rapid expansion of higher education, relative to the demand for the higher educated in the labour market. Notwithstanding these developments, however, it is still the case that the labour market position of the higher educated is better than that of the less educated, though it is no longer without problems. The questions that need to be asked are:

Is this absorption problem of an only temporary nature?
Does a disadvantageous start in the labour market in terms of unemployment or job mismatch have only a temporary or a lasting effect?

Since 1990 the Research Centre for Education and the Labour Market carries out annual surveys of the labour market entry and subsequent careers of graduates from Maastricht University. These surveys include measurements at two points in time, the first about one year after graduation and the second about six years after graduation. The objective of this chapter is to determine for this group of graduates what the effects of unemployment and job mismatch one year after graduation are on earnings and the job match six years after graduation. In this context, job mismatch is defined as having a job below the level of university education or as having a job unrelated to the relevant or related field of education.

The structure of the remainder of this chapter is as follows: Section 2 gives a brief overview of the existing literature in the field of the transition process from school to work, and of the subsequent mobility processes. Section 3 presents a model specification and gives a description of the data set used. Section 4 gives an overview of our results and section 5 contains our conclusions.

THEORY

The literature distinguishes a number of theories with respect to mobility processes and careers. These theories differ, however, with respect to the effects of unemployment and mismatches during the period of labour market entry on the subsequent labour market careers. The *job search* theory traditionally assumes that individuals will try to maximise the utilisation of their potential and therefore search for the best job offer (Hamermesh and Rees 1984). However, this 'off-the-job' search process is costly, due to opportunity costs of leisure and 'out of pocket' costs. The basic assumption of job search theories is that individuals will remain unemployed until the costs of continued unemployment exceed the expected gains from continued searching. This search process typically explains why graduates will have a chance of being unemployed for a while after leaving school.

Job matching theories stress factors such as uncertainty and imperfect information when explaining the school-to-work transition process (Johnson 1972; Jovanovic 1979). Workers lack adequate information about jobs, while firms lack information about the workers' skills. This lack of information applies especially to newcomers to the labour market. The transition period is therefore characterised by a high rate of job-to-job mobility (Topel and Ward 1988). This job-to-job mobility can be regarded as a process of information accumulation, both with respect to a worker's skills and to his own preferences for certain types of jobs (MacDonalds 1982).

Neither job search theories nor job matching theories predict lasting negative effects of initial unemployment or mismatches. However, there are other theories that do point to negative effects in the long run, although for different reasons. From a *human capital* perspective (Becker 1964; Schultz 1961), long-term unemployment or mismatches may seriously affect a worker's productivity. Skills may become obsolete, especially for those trained for rapidly changing professions. Mismatches during the period of labour market entry or long-term unemployment may therefore have negative consequences for future careers.

From a *signalling* point of view (Spence 1973) long-term unemployment may have an equally negative effect on job prospects. Being unemployed may be regarded by firms as a negative signal of workers' abilities or motivation. This may in itself reinforce the probability of staying unemployed or being forced to accept lower level jobs. Alternatively, having rapid success in the labour market may cause future employers to regard these workers as 'stars', which again reinforces their future chances of promotion (Rosenbaum 1984).

Segmentation theories generally point to mobility restrictions in the labour market. Job opportunities then become dependent on the segment in which the worker is employed. Firm-internal labour markets in particular provide specific career opportunities (Doeringer and Piore 1971). Entrance to the internal labour market is restricted to the so-called 'ports of entry'. Passing this hurdle will therefore create career opportunities which are denied to those who work in secondary segments. However, segmentation can also take place along occupational career lines, as Spilerman (1977) has shown. The common feature in the segmentation approach is that jobs differ not only by content but also by access to opportunities. Some jobs give access to career opportunities, while others do not. Applied to the situation of young graduates, this can be translated into particular effects of early jobs on future labour market success.

DATA AND MODEL

Data were taken from the annual surveys of graduates from Maastricht University. These surveys are conducted about 1½ years after graduation, with a follow-up survey carried out 4½ years later, i.e. 6 years after graduation. For this analysis, we use the data of the 1990 cohort of graduates who were interviewed in the autumn of 1991 and spring of 1996. The survey includes graduates from four faculties: the Faculty of Medicine, the Faculty of Health Science, the Faculty of Law, and the Faculty of Economics and Business Administration.[20] The 1991 survey had a response rate of 78% and consisted of 397 respondents. The 1996 follow-up survey had a response rate of 52%. The number of graduates who responded to both surveys amounts to 239, equivalent to 47% of the original cohort (see Ramaekers 1997).

In 1991, 83% of the graduates who responded to both surveys held a job at the time of the interview while 7% were unemployed. The remaining 10% were primarily involved in full-time education. In 1996, 96% held a job at the time of the interview and nobody was unemployed. The analysis in this chapter concentrates on those who were either employed or unemployed in 1991, and who held a job in 1996. Respondents older than 35 were excluded from the analysis.

For the description of the transition period in the model below, we use a number of variables that relate to initial unemployment and job mismatches. One of these refers to the number of months that a graduate has been unemployed in the first year after graduation. Then there are a few variables that relate to the situation at the time of the interview. The first variable indicates the labour market status at the time of the interview in 1991. For those who held a job, the job is characterised by two features. The first indicates the employer requirements in terms of university-level education, while

---

[20]. For an exhaustive description of the 1990 cohort, see Ramaekers and Heijke (1993).

the second indicates whether the job requires a particular field of education that matches the individual's education or a related education. Using these three variables we construct four dummies to describe the situation at the time of the interview. The first indicates whether or not the respondent was unemployed. The second indicates whether the job held in 1991 was below university level. The third indicates a job at university level for which a different field of education was required. The final dummy (the reference category) indicates a job at university level within one's own or a related field of education.

In addition to unemployment and job (mis)match, a number of skills and personal characteristics are taken on board as control variables. We distinguish between the following human capital characteristics:

-    the number of years of work experience after graduation;
-    any additional training or education after university study;
-    taking or having completed a second-stage or post-graduate course;
-    previous education at higher vocational or university level;
-    administrative and/or relevant work experience during study
-    and graduation from a particular faculty.

All these characteristics are represented as dummy variables with the exception of work experience, which is measured in years. As personal characteristics we include gender and age.

The first equation below estimates the chances of graduates changing jobs between 1991 and 1996. As explanatory variables we use skills and personal characteristics, the job match after one year, the size of the company and the logarithm of the gross monthly earnings of the job in 1991. The latter variable corrects for the fact that higher earnings may contribute to the decision not to change jobs, however poor the job match. The equation provides estimates only for graduates who were in paid work in both, 1991 and 1996.

$$M = a_0 + a_1L_{t=1} + a_2LF_{t=1} + a_3\ln W_{t=1} + a_4 S_{t=1} + a_5X + e \qquad (1)$$

where:

M = a dummy variable indicating a change of jobs between 1991 ($t=1$) and 1996 ($t=6$) with 1=change and 0 otherwise.

$L_{t=1}$ = a dummy variable with value 1 if the graduate has a job below university level (at $t=1$) and 0 otherwise.

$LF_{t=1}$ = a dummy variable with value 1 if the graduate has a job at least at university level but outside his or her own/related field of education (at $t=1$) and 0 otherwise.

$\ln W_{t=1}$ =   natural logarithm of the gross monthly income at $t=1$.

$S_{t=1}$ = size of firm at t=1 (with 1= < 10 persons; 2=10-49 persons; 3=50-99 persons; 4= >100 persons).

X   = vector with personal and skills characteristics.

The dummy variables L and LF indicate whether a job mismatch has any effects on job changes in the first six years after graduation. Graduates with a job for which the employer requires at least university level education and within their own or a related field of education constitute the reference category.

Equation (2) and (3) provide some job match evidence six years after graduation. The two equations indicate which characteristics affect the probability of a job at university education level, and the probability of a job within one's own or a related field of education, respectively. Amongst other things, both equations contain information about graduate unemployment at time t=1.

$$LV_{t=6} = a_0 + a_1 IU_{t=1} + a_2U_{t=1} + a_3L_{t=1} + a_4LF_{t=1} + a_5X + e \qquad (2)$$
$$F_{t=6} = a_0 + a_1 IU_{t=1} + a_2U_{t=1} + a_3L_{t=1} + a_4LF_{t=1} + a_5X + e \qquad (3)$$

where
$LV_{t=6}$ = a dummy variable indicating a job at university level at time t=6 (LV=1) or below university level (LV=0).

$F_{t=6}$ = a dummy variable indicating a job within (F=1) or outside (F = 0) one's own or a related field of education at time t=6.

$IU_{t=1}$ = initial unemployment after graduation until t=1 (in months).

$U_{t=1}$ = a dummy variable indicating whether the graduate is unemployed at t=1 (U=1) or employed (U=0).

All other variables are defined as above.

To determine the effects of unemployment or job mismatch on the earnings of graduates we turn to an equation which explains the logarithm of the gross monthly earnings on the basis of unemployment in the first year after graduation and the quality of the job match after one year:

$$\ln W_{t=6} = a_0 + a_1 IU_{t=1} + a_2U_{t=1} + a_3L_{t=1} + a_4LF_{t=1} + a_5X + e \qquad (4)$$

where
$\ln W_{t=6}$ = natural logarithm of the gross monthly earnings of a full-time working week at t=6.

All other variables are defined as above.

As it stands equations (2), (3) and (4) neglect the effects of unobserved heterogeneity. Procedures have been suggested, however, to take account of the effect of selectivity bias (Heckman 1979; Green 1993). We will not follow these procedures, however, but we will take account of the unobserved heterogeneity by adding to model (4) the job match at t=6. The earnings equation can now be expressed as:

$$\ln W_{t=5} = a_0 + a_1 IU_{t=1} + a_2 U_{t=1} + a_3 L_{t=1} + a_4 LF_{t=1} + a_5 L_{t=6} + a_6 LF_{t=6} + a_7 X + e \quad (5)$$
where

$L_{t=6}$ =   a dummy variable with value 1 if the graduate has a job below university level at t=6 (0 otherwise)

$LF_{t=6}$ =   a dummy variable with value 1 if the graduate has a job at least at university level but outside his or her own/related field of education at t=6 (0 otherwise).

We need to note that the coefficients of unemployment and mismatch variables at time t=1 are in this case underestimated. However, the direction of the effects can be observed. As estimation method we use logistic regression for the first three equations. The earnings equations are estimated by means of least squares.

RESULTS

Tables 1 and 2 show a number of descriptive results. Because we are interested in the effects of initial unemployment and job mismatch on employment a few of years later, it needs to be borne in mind that we have only taken into consideration those graduates who belonged to the labour force both one year and six years after graduation.

Of all university graduates, 65 per cent held a job at university level and in the field which matched their field of education one year after graduation (see Table 1). By the time t=6 the percentage proportion of graduates with a job at university level and in a matching field of education increased slightly. The 16 per cent of graduates who held a job below university level at time t=1 were all working in an area outside their field of education. Only one out of eight graduates who were in paid employment held the same job both one year and six years after graduation. The other graduates changed jobs at least once between t=1 and t=6. During that period average earnings increased from DFL 3700 to DFL 5970.

Table 1: Descriptive results of the graduates who belonged to the labour force both one year and six years after graduation[a]

	group of selected graduates
job situation after one year	
% unemployed	8
% with a job below university level	16
% with a job at university level but outside one's own field	11
% with a job at university level and within one's own field	65
job situation after six years	

% unemployed	0
% with a job below university level	18
% with a job at university level but outside one's own field	9
% with a job at university level and within one's own field	73
job changing	
% with more than one job between one and six years after graduation	88
initial unemployment	
average initial unemployment in months	1.8 (3.2)
size of the firm one year after graduation	
% in firm with < 10 persons	12
% in firm with 10-49 persons	16
% in firm with 50-99 persons	8
% in firm with >= 100 persons	63
earnings	
average gross monthly earnings in DFL after one year	3696 (992)
average gross monthly earnings in DFL after six years	5973 (2427)
skills characteristics	
average number of years of work experience	2.9 (2.2)
% with additional training or education after graduation	44
% engaged in second-stage or post-graduate course	18
% having completed second-stage or post-graduate course	28
% with previous education at higher level	11
% with administrative experience during study	35
% with relevant work experience during study	59
% graduated from the Faculty of Medicine	26
% graduated from the Faculty of Health Science	34
% graduated from the Faculty of Law	25
% graduated from the Faculty of Economics and Business Administration	16
personal characteristics	
% male	40
average age in years at graduation	25 (2.4)

[a] standard deviations in brackets (if applicable)

By examining the kind of jobs held and the wages earned six years after graduation Table 2 gives a first impression of the long-term effects of initial unemployment and job mismatch on respective labour positions. Those who were unemployed one year after graduation or started in a job below university level have a much lower probability of ending up in a university level job than those who started in a university-level job in the first place.

Table 3 shows the estimation results of the odds of changing jobs at least once between t=1 and t=6[21]. According to this analysis, working in a firm with 50 to 100 persons leads to lower mobility compared to those working in firms of other sizes. More work experience leads to a higher job mobility. This may be due to the search process and what the graduates consider to be the 'right' job. Being engaged in a second-stage or post-graduate course appears to have a negative effect on job mobility. Finally, graduates from the Faculty of Law change jobs less often than graduates from the Faculty of Economics and Business Administration - a result which may indicate the dynamic nature of modern business positions.

Table 2:Descriptive results of some different groups of graduates with respect to the job match and earnings six years after graduation

	Job match after six years			
Situation after one year	Job below university level (in %)	At university level but outside relevant work area (in %)	At university level and with relevant work area (in %)	Average earnings after six years (in DFL)
Unemployed	44	13	44	4359
Job below university level	60	7	33	5326
Job at university level but outside relevant work area	14	23	64	5946
Job at university level and with relevant work area	4	7	89	6299

---

[21]. This is of course only estimated for graduates who are in paid work at t=1 and t=6.

Table 3
Parameter estimates for job changing (standard errors between brackets)

	job changing (eq. 1)	
job match situation after one year		
a job below university level[a]	-0.232	(0.853)
a job at university level but outside one's own field[a]	1.021	(1.247)
firm size		
size of company	-0.097	(0.370)
initial unemployment		
initial unemployment	0.344	(0.290)
earnings after one year		
logarithm of gross monthly earnings	0.481	(1.354)
skills characteristics		
number of years of work experience	0.902**	(0.274)
additional course or education after graduation	1.204	(0.866)
engaged in second-stage or post-graduate course	-4.027**	(1.641)
completed second-stage or post-graduate course	0.518	(1.128)
previous education at higher level	0.480	(1.093)
administrative experience during study	0.352	(0.783)
relevant work experience during study	-1.156	(0.920)
graduated from the Faculty of Medicine[b]	2.997	(1.898)
graduated from the Faculty of Health Science[b]	-1.229	(1.426)
graduated from the Faculty of Law[b]	-2.899*	(1.501)
personal characteristics		
female[c]	-2.406**	(1.179)
age	-0.328	(0.205)
constant	10.488	(11.788)
number of cases	153	
-2 log likelihood	63.840	

[a] graduates with a job at university level and within their own or related field of education constitute the reference group

[b] graduates from the Faculty of Economics and Business Administration constitute the reference group

[c] male is the reference group

* significantly deviating from zero with a significance level of 10%

** significantly deviating from zero with a significance level of 5%

Table 4 shows the estimation results for the job match at time t=6 and the effects of unemployment and job mismatch at time t=1. The symbol ∞ for the dummy which refers to graduation from the Faculty of Medicine indicates that in the field of medicine there is an infinitely large chance of finding a job at university level and in the matching field of education.[22] Being unemployed or having a job which does not require university education has significant negative effects on the odds of finding a job at university level five years later (equation 2). We did not find any negative effects of these two variables on the odds of having a job related to one's field of education (equation 3). Here starting in a job not related to one's field of education has a lasting effect.It was also found that having taken previous education at a higher educational level has a significant negative effect on the probability of getting a job at university level. This can be explained by the fact that this group consists almost entirely of graduates who had previously taken higher vocational education. This group thus appears to have found work at higher vocational level, rather than at university level.

We now estimate equations (2) and (3) again, this time excluding the graduates who had the same jobs at times t=1 and t=6. This means that only those graduates who were unemployed at t=1 or graduates who changed jobs at least once between 1991 and 1996 are included in our analysis. The new results are shown in Table 5. The symbol ∞ again denotes an infinitely large effect of the variables in question.

Table 4
Parameter estimates for the job match six years after graduation (standard errors in brackets)

	level (eq. 2)		field (eq. 3)	
job situation after one year				
unemployed	-2.423**	(1.046) -	0.666	(1.172)
a job below university level[a]	-3.659**	(0.829)	-0.303	(1.238)
a job at university level but outside one's own field[a]	-1.517	(0.940)	-2.138**	(0.946)
initial unemployment				
initial unemployment	-0.093	(0.083)	-0.006	(0.113)
skills characteristics				
number of years of work experience	0.101	(0.142)	-0.102	(0.155)
additional course or education after graduation	0.035	(0.610)	-0.218	(0.779)
engaged in second-stage or post-graduate course	1.424	(1.386)	0.907	(1.202)
completed second-stage or post-graduate course	0.447	(0.680)	0.299	(0.925)
previous education at higher level	-2.191**	(1.076)	0.527	(1.479)
administrative experience during study	-0.845	(0.594)	-0.091	(0.760)

---

[22]. This means that after controlling for other variables almost all graduates of Medicine have a matching job. In order not to affect the other parameter estimates, this group has been left out in the analysis. This did not affect the estimated coefficients of the other variables.

relevant work experience during study	-0.362	(0.617)	0.257	(0.798)
graduated from the Faculty of Medicine[b]	∞		∞	
graduated from the Faculty of Health Science[b]	0.006	(0.954)	-2.714**	(1.309)
graduated from the Faculty of Law[b]	-0.332	(0.933)	-0.801	(1.301)
personal characteristics				
female[c]	0.600	(0.715)	1.056	(0.913)
age	0.168	(0.182)	0.178	(0.220)
constant	-1.495	(4.655)	-1.993	(5.533)
number of cases	131		101	
-2 log likelihood	92.696		70.323	

[a] graduates with a job at university level and within their own or related field of education constitute the reference group

[b] graduates from the Faculty of Economics and Business Administration constitute the reference group

[c] male is the reference group

* significantly deviating from zero with a significance level of 10%

** significantly deviating from zero with a significance level of 5%

Comparing Table 5 to Table 4, we see that at time t=6 the same variables show significant effects on the odds of holding a job at university level and in the appropriate field of education. Calculating the effects in terms of changes in the probability of finding a job at university level shows that being unemployed leads to a decrease of 4 percentage points. For the effect of holding a job below university level the decrease amounts to 7 percentage points. We refrain from further probability analyses. It should suffice to conclude that both unemployment and job mismatch at t=1 correlate with the later job match at t=6.

Table 5
Parameter estimates for the job match six years after graduation excluding graduates with the same jobs at t=1 and t=6 (standard errors in brackets)

	level (eq. 2)		field (eq. 3)	
job situation after one year				
unemployed	-2.123**	(1.044)	-0.485	(1.355)
a job below university level[a]	-3.559**	(0.927)	∞	
a job at university level but outside one's own field[a]	-1.318	(0.971)	-2.619**	(1.222)
initial unemployment				
initial unemployment	-0.082	(0.084)	0.025	(0.134)
skills characteristics				

number of years of work experience	0.195	(0.162)	-0.279	(0.214)
additional course or education after graduation	0.325	(0.659)	-0.277	(0.990)
engaged in second-stage or post-graduate course	0.818	(1.432)	0.879	(1.381)
completed second-stage or post-graduate course	0.918	(0.724)	-0.424	(1.100)
previous education at higher level	-2.251*	(1.180)	0.185	(1.866)
administrative experience during study	-0.713	(0.667)	1.055	(1.167)
relevant work experience during study	-0.399	(0.658)	-0.061	(0.997)
graduated from the Faculty of Medicine[b]	∞		∞	
graduated from the Faculty of Health Science[b]	0.078	(0.973)	-4.180**	(1.706)
graduated from the Faculty of Law[b]	-0.660	(0.976)	-0.767	(1.632)
personal characteristics				
female[c]	0.340	(0.744)	1.842	(1.219)
age	0.116	(0.189)	0.369	(0.339)
constant	-0.498	(4.792)	-6.168	(8.330)
number of cases	107		75	
-2 log likelihood	79.459		46.962	

[a] graduates with a job at university level and within their own or related field of education constitute the reference group

[b] graduates from the Faculty of Economics and Business Administration constitute the reference group

[c] male is the reference group

* significantly deviating from zero with a significance level of 10%

** significantly deviating from zero with a significance level of 5%

The results of the estimates on future earnings are given in Table 6. The first column shows the results of equation (5) including those graduates whose jobs were identical at times t=1 and t=6, respectively. The second column excludes this group of graduates. The table shows that being unemployed one year after graduation has a significant negative effect on later earnings. This cannot be explained by a lack of work experience in comparison with those who did not experience unemployment, since we explicitly control for the number of years of working experience after graduation. The number of months of unemployment has no significant effect. What appears to be of significance, however, is evidence of paid employment one year after graduation.

Table 6
Parameter estimates for earnings six years after graduation (standard errors in brackets)

	earnings (eq. 4) all graduates	earnings (eq. 4) excluding graduates with job t=1 equal to job t=6
job situation after one year		
unemployed	-0.299** (0.102)	-0.316**(0.109)
a job below university level[a]	-0.085 (0.073)	-0.124 (0.087)
a job at university level but outside one's own field[a]	0.070 (0.094)	0.088 (0.106)
initial unemployment		
initial unemployment	-0.007 (0.009)	-0.007 (0.009)
skills characteristics		
number of years of work experience	0.007 (0.012)	0.007 (0.014)
additional course or education after graduation	0.031 (0.054)	-0.022 (0.062)
engaged in second-stage or postgraduate course	-0.147* (0.078)	-0.165* (0.087)
completed second-stage or post-graduate course	0.176** (0.065)	0.166**(0.071)
previous education at higher level	-0.092 (0.090)	-0.017 (0.112)
administrative experience during study	-0.048 (0.053)	-0.092 (0.059)
relevant work experience during study	0.027 (0.054)	0.037 (0.058)
graduated from the Faculty of Medicine[b]	-0.112 (0.090)	-0.102 (0.098)
graduated from the Faculty of Health Science[b]	-0.120 (0.081)	-0.108 (0.090)
graduated from the Faculty of Law[b]	-0.123 (0.087)	-0.033 (0.100)
personal characteristics		
female[c]	0.042 (0.056)	0.072 (0.061)
age	0.038** (0.013)	0.050**(0.016)
constant	7.697**(0.336)	7.376**(0.395)
number of cases	155	134
adjusted R-square	0.167	0.194

[a] graduates with a job at university level and within their own or related field of education constitute the reference group

[b] graduates from the Faculty of Economics and Business Administration constitute the reference group

[c] male is the reference group

* significantly deviating from zero with a significance level of 10%

** significantly deviating from zero with a significance level of 5%

Table 7

Parameter estimates for earnings six years after graduation including the job match after six years (standard errors in brackets)

	earnings (eq. 5) all graduates	earnings (eq. 5) excluding graduates with job t=1 equal to job t=6
job situation after one year		
unemployed	-0.253**(0.104)	-0.263**(0.109)
a job below university level[a]	-0.025 (0.081)	-0.050 (0.095)
a job at university level but outside one's own field[a]	0.102 (0.097)	0.135 (0.108)
job match after five years		
a job below university level[a]	-0.163**(0.080)	-0.221**(0.088)
a job at university level but outside one's own field[a]	-0.010 (0.089)	0.001(0.107)
initial unemployment		
initial unemployment	-0.005 (0.009)	-0.004 (0.009)
skills characteristics		
number of years of work experience	0.006 (0.012)	0.004 (0.014)
additional course or education after graduation	0.028 (0.054)	-0.030 (0.062)
engaged in second-stage or post-graduate course	-0.156**(0.078)	-0.179**(0.085)
completed second-stage or post-graduate course	0.173**(0.065)	0.150**(0.071)
previous education at higher level	-0.049 (0.092)	0.058 (0.113)
administrative experience during study	-0.037 (0.053)	-0.084 (0.059)
relevant work experience during study	0.028 (0.054)	0.037 (0.057)
graduated from the Faculty of Medicine[b]	-0.113 (0.089)	-0.098 (0.097)
graduated from the Faculty of Health Science[b]	-0.116 (0.082)	-0.106 (0.091)
graduated from the Faculty of Law[b]	-0.128 (0.087)	-0.019 (0.099)
personal characteristics		
female[c]	0.034 (0.055)	0.068 (0.060)
age	0.036**(0.013)	0.047**(0.016)
constant	7.765**(0.335)	7.468**(0.391)
number of cases	154	133
adjusted R-square	0.184	0.229

[a] graduates with a job at university level and within their own or related field of education constitute the reference group

[b] graduates from the Faculty of Economics and Business Administration constitute the reference group

[c] male is the reference group

* significantly deviating from zero with a significance level of 10%

** significantly deviating from zero with a significance level of 5%

The size of the foregone earnings as a result of unemployment at time t=1 can be determined by the estimated coefficients. Being unemployed at time t=1 leads to a decrease in log earnings of 0.299. This means that gross earnings decrease by 1-exp(-0.299) or 26 per cent. Excluding the graduates who hold the same job at t=1 and t=6, leads to a similar decrease of 27 per cent. Whether a graduate has a job at university level or within a matching field of education one year after graduation has no significant effect on future earnings. Taking a second-stage or post-graduate course, however, is important. Initially, being engaged in such a course leads to lower earnings. However, returns to further education become evident after completion of the course. Age also has a positive effect on earnings. Compared to graduates of the Faculty of Economics and Business Administration, graduates of the Faculty of Health Science, the Faculty of Medicine and the Faculty of Law receive, on average, lower earnings after five years, although the effects are statistically insignificant.

We finally include the job match at time t=6 in the earnings equation. The results are listed in Table 7. The second column again excludes those graduates who held the same job at t=1 and t=6. The results in this table appear to be fairly similar to those in Table 6. However, the introduction of the job match at time t=6 leads to a significant improvement of the model. The value of the estimated coefficients which indicate the labour market status at time t=1 implies that unemployment leads to a fall in earnings of over 20 per cent at time t=6. We can also conclude that an initial job mismatch has no effect on later earnings, but does have an effect on future job matches.

CONCLUSION

Labour market developments immediately after graduation matter. Our study concludes that both youth unemployment and educational mismatch have a negative effect on future careers, future matches and, in the case of unemployment, on future earnings. These results are not predicted in the job search and job match theories and point to some lasting effects of labour market entry on careers later in life. It is also important to note, however, that some initial occupational mobility does not necessarily point to negative labour market experiences, mismatch or potential future unemployment. What it does show, however, is that the first few years in the labour market constitute an exploratory phase, in which graduates "shop around" and seek further labour market information. Graduates do not immediately find the jobs which properly match their education - a result that is in line with traditional job search and job matching theories.

REFERENCES

Becker, G.S. (1964), *Human Capital: A Theoretical and Empirical Analysis, With Special Reference to Education*, National Bureau of Economic Research, New York.

Doeringer, P.B. and M.J. Piore (1971), *Internal Labor Markets and Manpower Analysis*, Heath Lexington Books, Lexington.

Green, F. (1993), The Impact of Trade Union Membership on Training in Britain, *Applied Economics*, 25, pp. 1033-1043.

Greene, W.H. (1993), *Econometric Analysis*, second edition, Macmillan Publishing Company, New York.

Hamermesh, D.S. and A. Rees (1984), *The Economics of Work and Pay*, Harper & Row, New York.

Heckman, J.J. (1979), Sample Selection Bias as a Specification Error, *Econometrica, 47*, pp. 153-161.

Johnson, T.J. (1972), *Professions and power*, London: Macmillan.

Jovanovic, B. (1979), Firm-Specific Capital and Turnover, *Journal of Political Economy*, pp. 1246-1260.

MacDonald, G.M. (1982), A Market Equilibrium Theory of Job Assignment and Sequential Accumulation of Information, *The American Economic Review*, 72-5, pp. 1038-1055.

Ramaekers, G.W.M. and J.A.M. Heijke (1993), *'Arbeidsmarktscanner Rijksuniversiteit Limburg: Basismeting cohort '90' [Labour Market Scanner Maastricht University: Basic Measurements 1990 Cohort]*, ROA-R-1993/1, Maastricht.

Ramaekers, G.W.M. (1997), *' Start van de loopbaan na de Universiteit Maastricht 1995/1996' [Start of a Career after Maastricht University 1995/1996]*, ROA-R-1997/6, Maastricht.

Rosenbaum, J.E. (1984), *Career mobility in a corporate hierarchy*, Orlando: Academic Press.

Schultz, T.W. (1961), "Investment in Human Capital", *American Economic Review*, vol. 51, pp. 1-17.

Spence, O.F. (1973), "Job Market Signalling", *Quarterly Journal of Economics*, pp. 355-374.

Spilerman, S. (1977), "Careers, labor market structure, and socio-economic achievement", *American Journal of Sociology*, vol. 83, no. 3, pp. 551-593.

Topel, R.H. and M.P. Ward (1988), *Job Mobility and the Careers of Young Men*, National Bureau of Economic Research, New York.

CHAPTER 9

WHAT HAPPENED TO THE LOST GENERATION? CHANGES IN THE LABOUR MARKET STATUS OF FINNISH YOUTH, 1980 - 1993

KARI NYYSSÖLÄ

INTRODUCTION

The transition from school to work is an important part of the process of achieving adult status. Traditionally, growing up has been associated with financial independence, moving away from the parental home, acquiring a profession and a job, and starting a family. Unemployment and unstable labour markets hinder and delay these achievements in one way or another. In the case of Finland's youth labour markets we can refer to a risk-sensitive model of work, characterised by part-time and temporary jobs, low wages and insecurity - a scenario that could be described as a "hiring and firing" mentality (Bosch et al. 1992). Other characteristic features of this model include frequent job changes and periodic unemployment spells experienced by young people. Thus unemployment has become a "normal" experience for young people and one that is an essential and possibly influential part of their employment history.

Unemployment becomes a serious problem when the period of unemployment is prolonged. The longer an individual is out of work, the more difficult it becomes to find a job. Duration, however, is only part of the picture. Unemployment experienced in youth increases the probability of periodic unemployment later in life (e.g. Lynch 1985, 1989; Jehoel-Gijsbers and Groot 1989; Hammer 1996). This points to the problem of marginalisation of young people, some of whom experience repeated spells of prolonged unemployment (Hammer 1996, p. 452). However, the interface between unemployment and marginalisation has many dimensions, and previous studies have not been able to give a precise answer to the question of whether earlier unemployment is in itself the main cause of an unstable employment history or whether it is other factors that are are more influential (Baker and Elias 1994, p. 242).

This chapter will deal with the effects of youth unemployment on later employment histories and career developments, following the employment history of one Finnish age cohort from 1980 to 1993. The study seeks to address the following three research questions:

Between 1980 and 1993 how has the labour market developed and which features are characteristic of different groups in the labour market?

How do unemployment in 1980 and marginalisation correlate with employment history?

How does unemployment in 1980 affect an individual's labour market status in 1993?

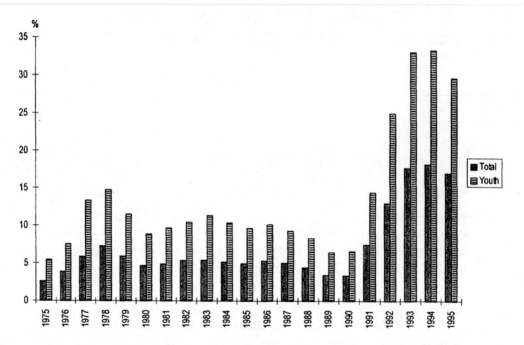

Figure 1: Total unemployment and youth unemployment rates in Finland 1975-1995 (%)

Source: SF 1996, p. 342.

The basic material for the study is taken from the 1970 census, taking a 40% random sample of all 3-5, 8-10, 13-15, 18-20, 28-30 and 33-35 year olds. The sample was conditional on the chosen individuals being included in later census material. The study therefore comprises a longitudinal analysis and combines observations in the census of 1970, 1975, 1980, 1985 and 1990, respectively. The material was supplemented by data from 1993 employment statistics. All in all, the material consists of 598,000 cases, and is in practice a representative sample of the working-age population of Finland today. Individuals who had been 18-24 years of age in 1980 were chosen for our analysis which provides us with a sample of 200,517 young people.

THE FACTORS BEHIND YOUTH UNEMPLOYMENT

In 1980, Finland was recovering from large-scale unemployment of the late 1970s. The immediate reason for the growth in unemployment can be traced back to the oil crisis and the ensuing recession, but at the same time Finland was also going through a process of structural change. In a decade or two, Finland had changed from a predominantly agricultural into an industrial and service-oriented society. With the increase in paid employment, unemployment had also become a permanent phenomenon. At the same time, youth unemployment became for the first time a widespread social problem.

In the late 1980s Finland's economic upswing coincided with a significant decrease in unemployment. In the 1990s, however, the economic upswing turned into recession once more and resulted in a dramatcic rise in unemployment. In 1993, total unemployment amounted to 17.9 per cent, with youth unemployment as high as 33.3 per cent. In 1994 the employment situation worsened. Only in 1995 did Finland experience a slight improvement in its unemployment statistics (see Figure 1).

It was not until the late 1970s that Finland's youth unemployment was seen as a considerable social problem. The term "the lost generation" came into use to describe the poor prospects of unemployed youth. Of course, back in the 1930s there were already some concerns about youth unemployment. What was new in the 1970s, however, was the fact that unemployment had been "socialised", i.e. it was declared a burning social issue mainly by the press and media and public commentaries. The most common implications of youth unemployment were seen in mental problems, loss of self confidence, the social isolation of young people, alcohol abuse, crime, unwillingness to work, inefficiency in job seeking and increased passivity (Siurala 1994).

The same debate was conducted in Great Britain in the early 1970s. The British were worried not only about the slackening work morale, but also that young people would "lose their grip on society" and thus fall prey to extreme political movements and crime. It was also feared that if young people found it difficult to enter the labour market, they would experience even greater difficulty later in life (Roberts 1995).

The growth of youth unemployment in the 1970s encouraged respective research activities, especially in Great Britain. At the same time research into the effects of youth unemployment also commenced in Finland. However, despite considerable research efforts no definite answer to the question of how youth unemployment affects the subsequent employment history has been found.

The subject can be approached from two different angles. First, spells of unemployment are seen as factors that reduce the likelihood of a young person finding employment. The view is based on the theory of human capital which regards work experience as a proxy of a worker's quality and productivity. In a recruiting situation, an employer considers spells of unemployment as a reduction of a worker's potential quality and productivity, which in turn reduces the probability of the individual's employment. As a result, a worker with an unfavourable work history may apply only for less skilled and less stable jobs - i.e. jobs in the secondary sector. This also worsens the job seeker's prospects of quality employment in the future, since it is generally more difficult to move from secondary sector employment into better jobs in the primary sector (Baker and Elias 1991, p. 216).

However, the human capital approach can be criticised in that it disregards other factors which may affect the recruitment decision, including social background variables, discrimination (sex, race, age etc.), wage differences, information asymmetry and other imperfections in the labour market. On the supply side job seekers may not always be able to assess their competencies realistically. They may aim either "too high" or "too low". It is important to make an optimal choice, however, since this choice is significant for a young person's later career (Ashton et al. 1990; Hammer 1996, p. 452). At times of high unemployment, however, young people may have to choose a labour market sector that does not match their training. As a consequence, such "mismatch" may have considerable negative effects on a young person's career development (Hammer 1996, p. 452) and it is argued that the human capital theory fails to take these possibilities into account.

With a second approach, however, help is at hand. In this model, unemployment on its own does not affect a worker's career. Instead, career devlopments are seen as being influenced by individual differences between people and various social factors (Baker and Elias 1991, p. 216). These individual differences may relate to work motivation, knowledge, skills and personality traits. Gender, education, colour of skin, place of birth and other family background variables are all factors which may affect an individual's chance to achieve a rewarding and fulfilling employment status.

THE RISKS OF MARGINALISATION

Many individual and social background factors are related to unemployment and an interrupted history of employment. It is these risk factors which contribute to economic and social marginalisation. Marginalisation originally referred to exclusion from the labour market, unemployment, incapacity and premature retirement. More recently, the term has been interpreted more widely by reference to different forms of disadvantage. In particular, some emphasis has been placed on a meaning which refers not only to economic exclusion but also to a more dynamic form of social disadvantage that continues to accelerate and grow over time.

Prior to Finland's current recession, various economic and social crises that affected people's lives were as a rule short-lived and of an only temporary nature. The central pillars on which people could build their lives included a relatively stable labour market, the wide if somewhat fragmented support net of the welfare state, and people's own families and other support networks. These structures acted as a kind of "filter" through which the ills of unemployment and other crises could be eliminated. Those individuals who did not have access to these filtering processes became Finland's focal problem group - marginal members of society - then and now, single working-class men living alone and often kept outside the support network of family and friends (Vähätalo 1996, p. 25).

Marginalisation may be passed down from one generation to the next. In Finland, it has been observed that of those adults on the receiving end of child welfare services to support the upbringing of their children, as many as 20 per cent have also as children been recipients of child welfare services (Kivinen 1994, p. 15). A similar phenomenon can be observed when we investigate the effect of social background on education. Success in the school system is closely linked with the child's family background (Kivinen and Rinne 1995). It thus comes as no surprise that it is mostly young people from working-class backgrounds who remain without appropriate school or vocational qualifications.

CHANGES IN LABOUR MARKET STATUS

A comparison of labour market status in 1980 and 1990 will be taken as our point of departure to examine young people's employment histories and respective career patterns. Table 1 shows that of the entire youth cohort those young people who were either in work or education in 1980 experience the most promising employment progression. Of each group, more than 70 per cent were still in employment in 1993. Ex-students appear to have an advantage over workers without academic experiences. In 1993, only 13 per cent of ex-students are without a job compared to 17 per cent of those who had been working in 1980 but didn't experience any further study. Youth unemployment seems to point to joblessness later in life, and this suprisingly often: only about half of those unemployed in 1980 are in employment in 1993 and a third are (still or again) unemployed.

Table 1: Labour market status of youth cohort[1] in 1980 and 1993

Status in 1980	Employment	Unemploy-ment	Student	Outside the Labour Force	Total	N
Employed	73	17	3	7	100	107253
Unemployed	49	34	3	14	100	7577
Student	75	13	5	8	101	54982
Outside the Labour Force	60	22	3	15	100	27896
Total	71	17	4	9	101	197708

[1] The labour market status was defined according to a week long cut-off point at the end of the year under study.

Table 2: Labour market changes by average accrued[2] income and unemployment months, and shares of unemployed in 1990 and 1985

Labour market status change 1980 to 1993	Avarage accrued Income (FIM)	Avarage accrued months of unemployment (m)	Share of unemploy-ment 1990 (%)	Share of unemploy-ment 1985 (%)	N
Employment to Employment	362237	1.1	1.5	2.4	77892
Employment to Unemployment	276808	10.6	15.4	9.7	18698
Unemployment to Employment	264412	9.1	5.0	12.0	3691
Unemployment to Unemployment	176667	21.7	26.9	30.6	2558
Student to Employment	342337	0.9	1.2	2.8	41135
Student to Unemployment	229554	9.6	12.1	9.4	7085

[2] Accrued income is the sum of income for the years studied, indexed to correspond to the 1994 value. The accrued months of unemployment are the sum of the months during which the individual was unemployed in the years studied.

In what follows we shall look more closely at the different transitory patterns between 1980 and 1993. Six different transitions can be identified:

- from employment to employment,
- from employment to unemployment,
- from unemployment to employment,
- from unemployment to unemployment,
- from study to employment and
- from study to unemployment.

The most interesting results come to the fore when we examine changes in average accrued income, months of unemployment and labour market status in 1985 and 1990, respectively.

Our income and unemployment observations indicate that those individuals who have developed positive transitory patterns have experienced employment/employment and study/employment transitions. For those groups average accrued income amounts to approximately FIM 350,000 (£50, 000) and the total average unemployment spell does not exceed one month. It should be noted, however, that the accrued income of those who have experienced study/employment transitions is actually higher than stated because they have worked fewer working years than those who experienced an employment/employment transition. Those individuals who have experienced unemployment/employment transitions have also achieved some reasonable improvements. Average accrued income amounts to about FIM 276,000 (approximately £40,000). It is interesting to note that for those individuals who experienced employment/unemployment transitions over the said period average accrued income rose to a similar level, amounting to FIM 264,000 (approximately £38,000). For those who went from study into unemployment, however, accrued average income amounts to only FIM 230,000 (approximately £31,000). This amount hardly justifies their investment in education, even though we need to bear in mind that the period of study has shortened the time they spent in employment and reduced their accrued income accordingly.

It comes as no surprise that those individuals who remained unemployed experienced the most severe financial shortfalls. Average accrued income amounts to a mere FIM 180,000 (approximately £26,000) over the said period and average unemployment spells amount to 22 months. This group can justifiably be called the "lost generation" - a group of youngsters who at no point entered the primary labour market or experienced any kind of career progression.

YOUTH UNEMPLOYMENT AND LABOUR MARKET STATUS IN 1993

Table 1 has shown that unemployment in 1980 correlates with the labour market status in 1993. We now want to examine how far the employment status in 1980 affects the labour market status when other background factors are taken into consideration. The method of analysis used is logistic regression, with "employment status in 1993" as our dependent variable and sex, age, education, marital status, place of residence, social background, accrued income and months of unemployment experienced in the years 1980, 1985 and 1990 as our explanatory variables. The parameter estimates used in the model are shown in Table 3.

With our parameter variables it is possible to calculate the average likelihood of employment at different points on the regression curve. As for our categorical variables respective values are calculated for different groups. The result is the average (percentage-proportional) likelihood of being employed (as compared to unemployed) in 1993. The regression curve profile shows how the likelihood varies with given values.

The likelihood of employment based on our categorical variables is shown in Table 4. The most decisive factor is sex: women are 13 per cent more likey to be employed than men. Other categorical variables are considerably less important, but do indicate a trend. Individuals with a good education have an advantage over the poorly educated, as have those with families over those living alone. Children from white collar and entrepreneurial backgrounds seem to do slightly better than those from blue collar or farming backgrounds. Place of residence is divided into two classes: Uusimaa (the province in which the capital of Finland is situated) and the rest of the country. The division is based on the fact that more than half of Finland's population live in Uusimaa. Uusimaa is also the most afluent region of the country, and unemployment has traditionally been lowest in mainland Finland. It thus is rather surprising that the likelihood of Uusimaa residents being employed is slightly lower than for the rest of the country. The difference is, however, negligible.

Table 3: Variables and parameter estimates (Maximum Likelihood Estimates) of the logistic regression model

	Parameter Estimate	Pr > Chi-Square
Intercept	-0.3099	0.0001
Sex	0.7216	0.0001
Age (in 1980)	-0.0535	0.0001
Marital status	0.2692	0.0001
Education	0.2615	0.0001
Months of unemployment 1980	-0.0421	0.0001
Months of unemployment 1985	-0.0672	0.0001
Months of unemployment 1990	-0.3255	0.0001
Social background	0.4175	0.0001
Place of residence	-0.0746	0.0001
Accrued income	7.25E-6	0.0001
- 2 LOG Likelihood	138060.85	
Likelihood Ratio Index (R^2)	17,52	

Dependent variable "Labour market status in 1993" : 1 = Employment, 0 = Not employment

Figure 2 shows that months of unemployment in 1980 and 1985 affect the likelihood of being employed in 1993 only marginally. Six months of unemployment in 1980 reduces the likelihood of being employed by four percentage points and twelve months of unemployment reduced the likelihood by ten percentage points. The corresponding figures for 1985 are only a little higher - 6 and 15 percentage points, respectively. The most important factor appears to be unemployment in 1990. If an individual has been unemployed for six months in 1990, the likelihood of being employed in 1993 is only 37 per cent. After one year of unemployment in 1990, this likelihood is reduced to only 7 per cent.

Table 4: Likelihood of employment in 1993 by sex, education, marital status, social background and place of residence (%)

SEX	
Female	83.0
Male	70.4
EDUCATION	
Comprenhensive schooling only	73.3
Vocational training	78.1
MARITAL STATUS	
Living alone	73.0
Living with family	77.9
SOCIAL BACKGROUND	
Father blue collar or farmer	73.7
Father white collar or entrepreneur	81.0
PLACE OF RESIDENCE	
Uusimaa	76.2
Other	77.5

Income has some relevance at the lower end of the accrued income scale. For example, at the level of FIM 100,000 (approximately £14,000), growth in accrued income increases the likelihood of employment by 2.3 percentage points. At higher income levels the effect of accrued income is less pronounced. Age does not appear to have much effect on the likelihood of employment. On average, younger age groups seem to fare slightly better than groups of older individuals, though the difference is marginal.

Our regression model levels out some of the results presented in Table 1: when other factors affecting employment are taken into consideration, unemployment in 1980 has little significance for the individual's situation in 1993. The risk of unemployment has increased largely by being unemployed in 1990, i.e. at a time of relatively low unemployment in Finland.

Figure 2: Likelihood of being employed in the year 1993 as a function of months of unemployment in 1980, 1985, 1990 (%)

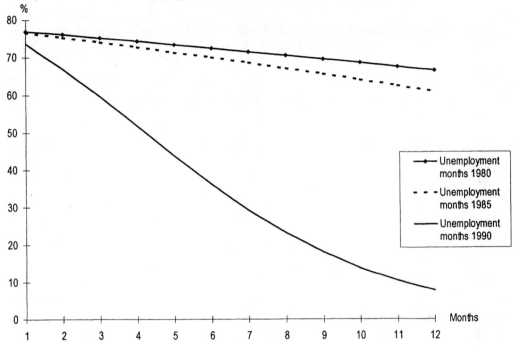

Sex remains a significant factor. Women have, on average, better employment prospects than men. This is also supported by general labour market statistics. In 1995 unemployment amounts to 16.7 per cent for women and 17.6 per cent for men. Women's labour market flexibility has been held up as a potential explanation (Hammer 1996). When faced with unemployment, it seems that women more readily place themselves outside the workforce than men.

YOUTH UNEMPLOYMENT AND MARGINALISATION

It is difficult to give an accurate definition of marginalisation. Some commentators concentrate on economic consequences, others highlight the implications for social policy. However, both groups use statistically measurable risk factors as explanatory variables, including unstable employment histories, recipientship of supplementary benefits, age, lack of vocational skill and education, male sex, lack of family support and social and financial deprivation.

In this study, the risk of marginalisation is measured by four variables: lack of education, male sex, one-person residency and working class family background. The most interesting results were obtained when only those young people who had been unemployed in 1980 were examined. In addition, our study looks closely at the "hard core" of the lost generation i.e. those who were still unemployed in 1990. The results are then compared with statistical averages for the whole youth cohort (see Table 5).

Table 5: Shares of youth cohort and of different groups by marginalization risk factors (%)

	Share of uneducated	Share of male	Share of living alone	Share of working class family	N
Youth cohort	20.1	51.1	15.3	55.1	200517
Unemployment to Employment	23.2	52.3	13.3	60.8	3691
"Lost Generation"	38.2	58.5	22.9	69.0	2558
"Hard core"	44.7	66.2	28.2	72.3	687

Table 5 shows that the relevant percentage proprotions are distinctly higher than average for the "lost generation" category. For the "hard core" of this group, the percentage proprotions depicting marginalisation are particularly high. Almost half of them lack education, two thirds are men, more than one fourth live alone and three quarters are from working class families. The marginalisation of the "hard core" is highlighted by the fact that they were on average unemployed for 7 months per year and that their accrued income was only about half of the average of the whole youth cohort.

On the basis of these results, it is evident that there is a small group of young people who are faced with an accumulation of economic and social problems. The statistics used do not show, however, whether these problems have led to marginalisation or to membership of a new societal underclass. Such causal links cannot be proven. What can be said, however, is that our empirical results give some strong indications that a weak labour market status is associated with economic and social unease.

CONCLUSION

The analysis above reveals a worrying statistic: a third of young people who were unemployed in 1980 had difficulty in gaining a strong foothold in the labour market later in life. It is, however, too simplistic to draw the conclusion that unemployment early in a person's working life automatically leads to negative implications for his or her career development. This study shows that lack of success in the labour market is associated with a number of other risk factors prognosticating economic and social marginalisation. Periodic unemployment on its own is not a direct cause of an unsuccessful employment history, but rather a consequence of an individual's lack of control over his or her own life course.

The process that leads to exclusion from work and an unstable work history can be very lenghty indeed and often begins in youth. For this reason, the employment status in 1980 does have some significance as the onset of a path leading to cumulative problems today, even though the regression analysis did not bring out these effect unambiguously.

Is there cause to worry about youth unemployment? Probability statistics alone predict that some young people today will turn into the lost generation of the future. There is cause to be concerned about those who in addition to unemployment face other problems associated with marginalisation. Fortunately, these young people form a small minority.

However, we face a more serious problem when it comes to the diagnosis of the risks and uncertainties of the modern labour market. A few decades ago, unemployment was often only temporary and frictional in nature and many youngsters went on to enter full-time permanent employment. Today, jobs are changing at a rapid pace and all too often lead to job insecurities, low wages and fixed-term contracts. Success in the labour market will depend more and more on the ability to change tack quickly and to adapt to rapidly changing job descriptions in a world of short-term, uncertain work relations (Grotenhuis and Meijers 1994, p. 229). Uncertainty and short-termism appear to be part and parcel of the changing nature of work. In future, employees will be expected to show more adaptability and flexibility. If the readiness to meet this challenge is absent, however, the risk of marginalisation will continue to grow.

REFERENCES

Asthon, D., Maguire, M. and Spilsbury, M. (1990), *Restructuring the Labour Market: The Implications for Youth*, MacMillan, London.

Baker, M. and Elias, P. (1991), "Youth unemployment and work histories" in S. Dex (ed.), *Life and Work History Analyses: Qualitative and Quoantitative Developments*, London: Routledge, pp. 214-244.

Bosch, G. , Dawskins, P. and Michon, F. (1992), *Working Time in Fourteen Industrialised Countries: An Overview*, Gelsenkirchen, Institut Arbeit und Technik.

Grotenhuis, H. and Meijers, F. (1994), "Societal cosequences of youth unemployment" in A.C. Petersen and J.T Mortimer (ed.), *Youth Unemployment and Society*, Cambridge: University Press, pp. 227-247.

Hammer, T. (1996), "Concequence of Unemployed in the Transition from Youth to Adulthood in a Life Course Perspective", *Youth & Society*, vol. 27, no. 4, pp. 450-468.

Jehoel-Gijsbers, G. & Groot, W. (1989), "Unemploued Youth: A Lost Generation?", *Work, Employment & Society*, vol. 3, no. 4, pp. 491-508.

Kivinen, T. (1994), *Valikoituminen lastensuojelun asiakkaaksi: Näkökulmia asiakkuuden määrittelemiseen*, Helsinki, STAKES.

Kivinen, O. and Rinne, R. (1995), *Koulutuksen periytyvyys: Nuorten koulutus ja tasa-arvo Suomessa*, Helsinki, Statistics Finland.

Lynch, L. (1985), "State Dependency in Youth Unemployment - A Lost Generation?", *Journal of Econometrcis*, vol. 28, April, 72-84.

Lynch, L. (1989), "The youth labor market in the eighties: determinants of re-employment probabilities for young men and women", *Review of Economics and Statistics*, vol. 71, no. 1, pp. 37-45.

Roberts, K. (1995), *Youth and Employment in Modern Britain*, Oxford University Press, Oxford.

SF (1996), *Statistical Year Book of Finland 1995*, Helsinki, Statistics Finland.

Siurala, L. (1994), *Nuoriso-ongelmat modernisaatioperspektiivissä*, Studies of the City of Helsinki.

Vähätalo, K. (1996), Pitkäaikaistyöttömät ja lamasta selviytyminen, *Studies on Labour Policy*, Ministry of Labour, No 132, Helsinki, Finland.

CHAPTER 10

RELIGION, EDUCATION, "FIRST DESTINATIONS" AND LATER CAREERS: THE PERSISTENCE OF INEQUALITIES IN NORTHERN IRELAND

IAN SHUTTLEWORTH

INTRODUCTION

The institutional, labour market, and educational contexts of youth transitions from school to work in Northern Ireland have changed markedly in the past two decades in common with trends in many other advanced economies. Key features have been a restructuring of the labour market that has resulted in a decline in employment for young people and government responses to increased education and training provision. The relatively short transitions that characterised the 1960s and the early 1970s have been replaced by longer, more complex, and more protracted transitions through a greater variety of educational, training, and employment statuses (Furlong 1992; Payne 1995; Roberts et al 1994).

These developments have posed policy questions about youth unemployment, education, training and equality in many countries. In Northern Ireland policymakers have confronted the same issues as their peers elsewhere. For example, as in Britain, the 1970s and 1980s saw the expansion of training provision and education in Northern Ireland in response to declining employment opportunities. There has been the same emphasis on providing "relevant" training, and the education and training system has largely followed the same trajectory as its British counterpart.

However, the political background of violent conflict (and continued sectarian competition since the start of the Peace Process) has added an extra dimension to labour market and social policy in Northern Ireland. This is because religious inequalities in the labour market have been perceived by some (see, for example, the discussion in McGarry and O'Leary 1995) to have been causes of "The Troubles". Because of this there has been a concern with employment equality. The removal of educational and labour market differentials between Catholics and Protestants is seen as a way of providing the preconditions for peace - or at least controlling conflict. Substantial legislative intervention has therefore attempted to achieve justice in the labour market. For example, to work toward "Fair Shares" in employment, the British government introduced Fair Employment Acts in 1976 and 1989 to establish the Fair Employment Agency (FEA) and to strengthen the powers of its successor, the Fair Employment Commission (FEC).

Young people[23] have not been an explicit and separate target for fair employment policy but an understanding of their fortunes is important in gauging the success of fair employment policy, other policy interventions in education and training, and future prospects for the Northern Ireland labour market. Firstly, as in other economies, the early post-school transition stage is an important predictor of later life chances. Secondly, the experience of young people can offer insights into how far the factors causing religious differentials are contemporary in their action. For example, differentials for males aged 40-50 could be dismissed as a result of past failings of the education system, past discrimination and past demographic background.

Because of this it is important to understand if, and how, religious differentials evolve for contemporary young people in a different economic, institutional and legislative situation than in the past. The chapter therefore examines religious differentials between Catholics and Protestants[24] in terms of economic restructuring and institutional change. Data from the 1971 and 1991 Censuses of Population are used to provide a 'long overview' of the issues and survey data of 1985 and 1991 school-leavers permits a more detailed examination. The next section begins the account by providing a brief overview of the economic and policy background in Northern Ireland to provide a context for the discussion.

THE BACKGROUND IN NORTHERN IRELAND

There are many reasons to expect that labour market and other differentials between young Catholic and Protestant people in Northern Ireland should have diminished during the 1970s and 1980s. The first set of factors relates to broad patterns of socio-economic and institutional change which have transformed post-school transitions in most advanced economies. The second set of factors are specific to Northern Ireland and refer to legislative changes to attempt to ensure justice in the labour market. There are many perspectives on socio-economic restructuring and fair employment legislation in Northern Ireland. A full account of these would be tedious and would perhaps generate more heat than light. However, some comments on the most salient features can usefully suggest some hypotheses for further examination.

---

[23] Defined very broadly as people aged 16-24 for the purposes of the chapter

[24] Defined as Protestants who stated they had a religion in response to Census of Population and survey questions. In practice, given the demographic structure of Northern Ireland, the vast majority of Protestants belong to a Protestant denomination.

Socio-economic change and the transformation of post-school transitions

Recent economic, social and institutional changes have restructured the Northern Ireland labour market in common with the labour markets of other advanced economies. The exact interpretation of this restructuring is contested and there are several competing theoretical perspectives[25]. Most accounts agree that there has been a substantial loss of (male) manufacturing jobs, a rise in female employment, and the growth of new kinds of 'flexible' work. The precise nature of these trends (and their theoretical interpretations) need not detain us here, but this process of labour market restructuring has led to fundamentally different labour market/educational opportunities for young people in the 1990s than in the 1970s or even the 1980s.

These mean that young people in the 1990s face very different opportunities (and constraints) than their peers in the 1980s and 1970s. Labour market change, and the collapse of industrial employment, has undoubtedly been one of the most important features. However, the growth of training and the expansion of education, while partly a response to labour market change (Ashton et al, 1990), have also been strong independent influences on the possibilities open to young people. Combined, the collapse of the youth labour market, (Hart, 1988), the inception of mass training schemes for 16-19 year olds, and the expansion of post-school education, has meant that transitions from school have ceased to be a simple move into work, but instead have become *protracted transitions* (Furlong, 1992) that can go through many stages of education, training, unemployment and employment before stability is achieved.

The concept of the *protracted transition* is worth further exploration. Broadly, it is argued that before the onset of labour market restructuring in the late 1970s and the early 1980s, the key event for most young people was the move from school into work. For many young people (excepting those who took A Levels and sought entry to higher education) this was the major influence on later social and labour market standing and a significant determinant of social stratification. The type of job entered and possible career prospects were mainly a function of the type of school attended and educational qualifications gained. This traditional type of transition was modified by the rise in unemployment, and the growth of training and post-compulsory education. These developments meant that the transition from school-to-work became less numerically significant, and indeed that rather than being the rule, quickly became the exception (see Payne, 1995 for details of trends in England & Wales during the 1980s and 1990s).

The greater variety of possible destinations has had two effects on young people. Firstly, there are a greater number of mediating destinations between school and entry to employment. These include training and further education and they might be assumed to give young people who perform poorly at school a 'second chance'. Secondly, most young people in the 1990s do not make an abrupt transition to employment at the age of 16; the majority finally gain employment after a succession of other experiences which means that the transition to work may last until the age of 19 (or even later) - and that even then there is no ultimate guarantee of success for some.

---

[25] See for example, Gertler (1988) on Post-Fordism and Bell (1973) on Post-Industrialism

The impact of the changes outlined is a matter of dispute. One side of the argument would suggest that the expansion of post-compulsory education and training effectively gives young people a 'second chance'. A more cynical argument would be that the collapse of youth employment enforces an 'equality of misery'. The other side of the debate, developed by Furlong (1992), contends that the protracted transition has had little real effect on life chances and that the ultimate labour market destinations of young people can be as accurately predicted today, given a knowledge of educational and social background, much as in the simpler transitions to work in the past.

In the Northern Ireland context it is suggested that many male manufacturing jobs, particularly in the heavy industry of the Belfast Urban Area (BUA), were largely dominated by Protestants and that the loss of these jobs has therefore disproportionately affected the Protestant community (see Cormack et al, 1980 for an early version of this argument). In a variety of the 'equality of misery' argument this might be assumed to have led to an equalisation of unemployment rates particularly since the process by which Protestant 'lads follow dads' into employment has now been disrupted. This analysis has been expanded upon with reference to new service employment which has been associated by some with the growth of a Catholic middle class (Smyth and Cebulla, 1995) and which could therefore also mean the lessening of labour market differentials.

Moreover, the institutional background in Northern Ireland has changed markedly in the past twenty years. The growth of training and post-compulsory education could be expected to have equalised 'human capital' between Protestants and Catholics and thus have removed one major source of labour market inequality (Cormack and Osborne, 1991) by giving many disadvantaged young people a 'second chance'. The increase in the proportion of young people gaining qualifications, together with the expansion of training and education, might also have led to greater credentialism as traditional routes into the labour market are destroyed by economic change.

Fair Employment Legislation in Northern Ireland

Socio-economic restructuring and institutional restructuring suggest profound changes in post-school transitions in Northern Ireland and possibly a radical closing of Catholic/Protestant differentials. A further reason for expecting a decrease in religious differentials is the expansion of fair employment legislation in Northern Ireland. This legislation is amongst the most far-reaching and proactive employment equality legislation in the United Kingdom (Cormack and Osborne, 1991).

Fair employment legislation is controversial and complicated to implement, and the path to the present legislation has been long and difficult (Rose and Magill, 1996). The genesis of fair employment can be traced to the Northern Ireland Civil Rights Movement of the 1960s which was an initial response to injustices in the distribution of housing but quickly expanded to challenge discrimination in public appointments and employment. It is a measure of the controversy associated with this issue in Northern Ireland that even now the existence of past discrimination (in the 1960s and earlier) is still hotly debated by both academics and politicians - as are interpretations of fair employment legislation.

The start of violence in 1969 gave a new context to civil rights and to employment issues particularly because socio-economic grievances were seen as being significant causes of violence and of Catholic alienation in particular. One consequence of the growth of violence was the abolition of the Northern Ireland Stormont Parliament and the introduction of Direct Rule from Westminster in 1972. An important policy objective following the start of Direct Rule was to remedy some of the socio-economic problems associated with the rule of the largely Unionist Stormont Parliament and the early and mid 1970s saw a variety of initiatives to reduce labour market discrimination. These culminated in the 1976 Fair Employment Act and the establishment of the FEA. Quotas to ensure that Catholics and Protestants had defined shares of employment were rejected in the 1976 Fair Employment Act and the principle of individual merit in employment was preserved. The FEA was responsible for enforcing the 1976 Fair Employment Act by making investigations of employers and examining complaints of discrimination.

By the early 1980s there were pressures to reform the 1976 Fair Employment Act. One source was a campaign which began in the United States and which promoted the MacBride Principles. This put employment equality back on the agenda not least because the incorporation of the MacBride Principles into state legislation and corporate practice in the United States meant problems in attracting inward investment to Northern Ireland. The 1985 Anglo-Irish Agreement (AIA) with its emphasis on accommodating the rights and identities of the 'two communities' in Northern Ireland gave additional impetus to further employment equality legislation.

The consequence of these external pressures for change, and the internal realisation by the British government that the unemployment differential remained, led to further reviews of the 1976 Act. This culminated in the 1987 Standing Advisory Commission on Human Rights (SACHR) Report, a 1988 White Paper and finally the 1989 Fair Employment Act which established the FEC (Fair Employment Commission). The FEC was a more powerful body than the FEA and its remit was to promote equality of opportunity in Northern Ireland, to promote affirmative action and to work toward the elimination of discrimination (Metcalf, 1996).

The FEC has many powers - all companies with more than 10 employees working more than 16 hours a week were required to register and large employers (with more than 250 employees) had give recruitment information. Moreover Section 31 of the 1989 Act meant that employers had to provide a review every three years of their workforce composition and recruitment practices. Means to enforce the provisions of the 1989 Act include an independent Fair Employment Tribunal which can instruct compensation to be paid to a complainant, contract compliance and grant denial.

It is important to realise that although the legislation is powerful in United Kingdom terms, it is employer focussed. It seeks only to ensure fair recruitment to jobs on individual merit although the acceptance of affirmative action can mean outreach to support the disadvantaged by, for example, the provision of appropriate training or the encouragement of job applications from under-represented communities. Despite this, the 1989 Fair Employment Act remains what it says - an act that deals with employment and the demand side of the labour market but which does not really consider the supply of labour and the broader causes of Catholic/Protestant differentials.

To investigate the impact of the themes of socio-economic restructuring and legislative change upon post-school outcomes, the chapter now looks at observed differentials between Catholic and Protestant young peoples. These are 'raw' observed differences as no attempt is made to control for the effects of religion after social composition and other background variables have been taken into account. The first, and more general view, is taken using data from the 1971 and 1991 Censuses of Population. The second, and more detailed perspective, focuses on the experiences of fifth-form school-leavers (largely 16 year olds) using data from the Youth Cohort Study (YCS) and the Secondary Education Leavers' Survey (SELS) during the 1980s and the 1990s.

AN OVERVIEW OF OBSERVED RELIGIOUS DIFFERENTIALS FOR YOUNG PEOPLE, 1971-1991

Tables 1 to 5 show selected dimensions of Catholic/Protestant differentials for young people aged 16-24 using tabulations from the 1971 and 1991 Censuses of Population. Each table presents data on the observed rates of, for example, educational participation for 1971 and 1991, the percentage point difference between Catholics and Protestants, and the ratio of the Catholic rate over the Protestant rate.

Table 1: Employment Rates (percentage of age group) for Catholics and Protestants 1971 and 1991

	1971				1991			
Age	Catholic	Protestant	Difference (pp)	Ratio	Catholic	Protestant	Difference (pp)	Ratio
16	39.4	41.0	-1.6	0.96	4.5	6.6	-2.1	0.68
17	53.3	55.7	-2.4	0.95	15.5	22.5	-7.0	0.69
18	63.3	64.8	-1.5	0.97	27.6	37.4	-9.8	0.73
19	66.6	70.4	-3.8	0.95	38.9	51.5	-12.6	0.75
20	67.7	70.9	-3.2	0.95	45.2	57.8	-12.6	0.78
21	65.4	70.6	-5.2	0.92	48.1	61.3	-13.2	0.78
22	66.1	71.9	-5.8	0.91	51.9	65.5	-13.6	0.79
23	64.4	72.0	-7.6	0.89	56.7	70.1	-13.4	0.80
24	63.7	70.4	-6.7	0.90	58.7	71.6	-12.9	0.81

Source: Census of Population 1971 and 1991

These data provide a cross-sectional 'before and after picture' of the labour market, educational and training experiences of young people. Because the Census of Population is not a sample the tables provide a description of the entire 16-24 resident Northern

Ireland population. In interpreting the tables two points should be borne in mind. Firstly, not everyone in Northern Ireland responds to the question on religion as this is voluntary. Secondly, higher rates of emigration of Protestants in 1991, particularly in connection with entry to higher education after the age of 18 may mean that the participation of Protestant young people as a whole in education might be underestimated. However, the focus of most social policy in Northern Ireland is on the resident population so the Census of Population is a useful science.

Table 2: Unemployment Rates (percentage of age group) for Catholics and Protestants 1971 and 1991

Age	1971				1991			
	Catholic	Protestant	Difference (pp)	Ratio	Catholic	Protestant	Difference (pp)	Ratio
16	5.3	2.8	2.5	1.89	5.5	4.6	0.9	1.19
17	7.0	3.7	3.3	1.89	8.0	6.1	1.9	1.31
18	9.3	4.8	4.5	1.93	14.4	10.8	3.6	1.33
19	9.8	5.1	4.7	1.92	19.6	13.2	6.4	1.48
20	11.0	5.3	5.7	2.07	19.7	12.4	7.3	1.58
21	11.9	5.3	6.6	2.24	20.1	12.3	7.8	1.63
22	11.2	4.8	6.4	2.33	20.6	12.2	8.4	1.68
23	10.7	4.4	6.3	2.43	20.9	12.7	8.2	1.64
24	10.3	4.3	6.0	2.39	20.1	11.8	8.3	1.70

Source: Census of Population 1971 and 1991

The simplest way to summarise the details in the tables is in terms of *absolute* and *relative* change. Absolute change is easier to describe because there are several major developments which mean that the position of young people in 1991 was very different to that in 1971. The first significant change is the massive decrease in employment rates noted in Table 1. Rates for 16 year olds declined from about 40% in 1971 to about 5% in 1991 - and these absolute falls have affected both Catholics and Protestants. Secondly, there has been a large growth in educational participation of between 20 to 30 percentage points (pp). This has been particularly marked for young people aged 16 to 18. Thirdly, training provides a new destination for young people in 1991 in comparison with people of the same age in 1971. Finally, unemployment increased between 8-10pp especially for those aged over 18 between 1971 and 1991. Tables 1 to 5 show some of the features noted in other advanced economies in that the importance of employment has decreased since many more young people tend now to enter education and training than in the past. The decline of employment and the growth of education and training is particularly important for young people aged under 18.

Table 3: Educational Participation (percentage of age group) for Catholics and Protestants 1971 and 1991

Age	1971				1991			
	Catholic	Protestant	Difference (pp)	Ratio	Catholic	Protestant	Difference (pp)	Ratio
16	50.5	53.0	-2.5	0.95	82.3	81.7	0.6	1.01
17	36.4	37.9	-1.5	0.96	59.7	55.2	4.5	1.08
18	23.9	26.3	-2.4	0.90	47.9	42.3	5.6	1.13
19	16.9	18.0	-1.1	0.94	33.6	28.7	4.9	1.17
20	12.7	14.6	-1.9	0.87	25.2	22.1	3.1	1.14
21	9.7	11.3	-1.6	0.86	20.5	17.6	2.9	1.16
22	6.3	7.5	-1.2	0.84	15.6	12.6	3.0	1.23
23	2.8	3.8	-1.0	0.73	7.9	6.0	1.9	1.31
24	1.6	2.3	-0.7	0.69	4.5	3.3	1.2	1.36

Source: Census of Population 1971 and 1991

Table 4: Inactivity Rates (percentage of age group) for Catholics and Protestants 1971 and 1991

Age	1971				1991			
	Catholic	Protestant	Difference (pp)	Ratio	Catholic	Protestant	Difference (pp)	Ratio
16	4.8	3.2	1.6	1.50	0.7	0.7	0.0	1.00
17	3.3	2.7	0.6	1.22	1.5	1.5	0.0	1.00
18	3.5	4.1	-0.6	0.85	2.6	3.1	-0.5	0.83
19	6.7	6.5	0.2	1.03	4.6	4.5	0.1	1.02
20	8.6	9.2	-0.6	0.93	6.7	6.2	0.5	1.08
21	12.9	12.8	0.1	1.01	9.0	7.7	1.3	1.16
22	16.5	15.8	0.7	1.04	10.1	8.6	1.5	1.17
23	22.1	19.7	2.4	1.12	12.8	10.3	2.5	1.24
24	24.3	22.9	1.4	1.06	15.1	12.4	2.7	1.21

Source: Census of Population 1971 and 1991

It is probable that an education or training effect masks unemployment and employment differentials for this group of young people. However, despite these significant absolute changes, relative differentials between Catholics and Protestants seem to be as important in 1991 as in 1971 although these relative differences by religion are difficult to describe because of the greater complexity of labour market and educational statuses in 1991. Looking first at Table 1, there is evidence that although employment rates have decreased markedly, especially for the under 20s, that the Catholic/Protestant employment differential has widened in terms of both the absolute percentage point difference and the ratio of Catholic to Protestant employment rates. This contradicts arguments about the expected result of deindustrialisation.

Table 5: Training Participation (percentage of age group) for Catholics and Protestants 1991

	1971				1991			
Age	Catholic	Protestant	Difference (pp)	Ratio	Catholic	Protestant	Difference (pp)	Ratio
16	-	-	-	-	7.0	6.3	0.7	1.11
17	-	-	-	-	15.2	14.0	1.2	1.08
18	-	-	-	-	7.6	6.3	1.3	1.20
19	-	-	-	-	3.3	2.2	1.1	1.50
20	-	-	-	-	3.1	1.5	1.6	2.06
21	-	-	-	-	2.3	1.2	1.1	1.91
22	-	-	-	-	1.9	1.1	0.8	1.73
23	-	-	-	-	1.8	1.0	0.8	1.80
24	-	-	-	-	1.6	0.9	0.7	1.77

Source: Census of Population 1991

Secondly, examining Table 2, the Catholic/Protestant ratio of unemployment rates has narrowed slightly between 1971 and 1991 which suggests that Protestant rates of unemployment have begun to catch up with Catholic rates in an 'equality of misery'. However, the percentage point difference widened. Finally, the social role of education appears to have changed (Table 3). In 1971, educational participation was higher for Protestants than Catholics for all single-year age groups but by 1991 this position was reversed with Catholics having educational participation rates some 3-4pp higher than Protestants.

These tables show that Catholic/Protestant differentials in labour market behaviour remain as salient in 1991 as in 1971 despite falling employment, rises in unemployment, the introduction of training, and the expansion of education. Indeed, in the case of employment, observed religious differentials have widened expressed both as a ratio and a percentage point difference. The key indicator of the ratio of unemployment rates shows some signs of narrowing but this might be because of other developments such as the expansion of educational participation. However, the greater complexity of youth transitions means that the issue is now not only one of unemployment and employment but also one of education and training since Catholic/Protestant differentials can also be observed for these statuses. The religious differential in educational uptake in favour of Catholics is intriguing and could suggest a changed role for education - and it might also suggest Protestant disadvantage. Greater rates of Catholic participation in education and training might offer prospects of reducing later labour market differentials by equalising human capital endowments. Alternatively, education and training might merely be new routes by which Catholic/Protestant inequality is reproduced immediately after leaving school and these differences might continue into later life because of inefficiencies and inequalities in education and training provision. More evidence is needed to differentiate between these viewpoints.

Data from the Census of Population are relatively inflexible. They merely provide 'snapshots' of the situation in 1971 and 1991 and little can be said about processes in intervening years. The cross-sectional nature of the Census data also restrict the questions that may be posed in that the experiences and post-school outcomes for a cohort of young people cannot be traced through time. Therefore, to begin to understand recent developments in more detail, and to gain this cohort perspective, the next section of the chapter uses the 1984 Youth Cohort Study (YCS) and the 1991 Secondary Education Leavers' Survey (SELS).

OBSERVED DIFFERENCES IN POST-SCHOOL TRANSITIONS

The YCS and the SELS offer a different cohort perspective in contrast to the cross-sectional Census of Population data. The SELS contains information on the educational, social and personal background of young people together with their 'first destination' in 1992 and their later destination in 1994. The YCS contains similar data to the SELS on the 'first destinations' of young people in 1985 and their subsequent destinations in 1987. To gauge the robustness of comparisons drawn between these data it is necessary to understand something of their structure and coverage, and the degree to which they are similar.

DATA STRUCTURE

The SELS was an *event cohort* randomly sampled from a population of all Northern Ireland school-leavers in 1990-91. Data on 'first destination' in April 1992 were collected along with school and home profile information. The sample was re-surveyed in the Autumn of 1994 to give data on 'final destination'. The YCS differs from the SELS in that it is an *age cohort* (rather than being an event cohort of all school-leavers) that traced the fortunes of a sample of young people. It commenced just before they reached the end of compulsory schooling at the age of 16 in the Spring of 1984 (collecting information on 'first destination in 1985) and continued to follow the cohort to the Winter of 1987 (McWhirter, 1989).

Because of the varying nature of the YCS and the SELS, direct comparisons cannot be made between the two surveys without adjustments. The SELS samples a population of all school-leavers whereas the YCS only samples 16-year olds some of whom had not left school. To achieve some degree of comparability only selected subsets of fifth-form school-leavers from both databases could be used. In practice this meant selecting fifth-form school-leavers from the SELS and selecting an analogous set of school-leavers from the YCS who had left school in the Spring and Summer of 1984. This limits the sample to a sub-set of school leavers and the conclusions drawn from it have to be tempered. However, the same types of differentials observed in the Census are also apparent for both the YCS and SELS.

The variables used as a measure of post-school outcomes were also coded to achieve a measure of comparability. The SELS and the YCS, for example, differed in their definition of unemployment and education. However, it proved possible to arrive at a common set of definitions (albeit at the expense of loosing detail) that permitted comparisons. A particular issue was unemployment. Following the many administrative changes in the definition of unemployment between 1984 and 1991, the simplest option was to define unemployment as a residual category (eg not in work, training or education). In practice this had little impact since the majority of the 'unemployed' were in fact out of work rather than in a miscellaneous status.

To summarise, the databases extracted from the YCS and the SELS hold data respectively on 1,244 young people who left school from fifth form in 1984, and 769 who left school from fifth form in 1991. The outcome variables used in the chapter to describe post-school outcomes were:

Outcomes at 'first destination' (April 1985 and April 1992 for the YCS and SELS datasets respectively) coded as employment, training, unemployment/other, and education

Outcomes at 'final destination' (October 1987 and October 1994 for the YCS and SELS databases respectively) coded again as employment, training, unemployment/ other, and education

The social and educational coverage of the SELS and YCS therefore differs from that of the complete coverage of the Census of Population. This has important implications for interpreting the SELS and YCS data. Basically, fifth-form school-leavers are a subset of all school-leavers as they are mostly aged 16. There is also no information on those who 'stay-on' at school because of the definition of the datasets. Given the structure of the Northern Ireland education system school-leavers at this age are more likely to be socially disadvantaged. They are therefore not representative of the wider social, educational, and labour market experiences of young people. Despite this caveat, it is interesting to examine the prevalence of religious disadvantage amongst this less socially-advantaged group not least because of the correlation often made between social deprivation, religious differentials and political mobilisation.

Observed differentials in post-school outcomes

Tables 6 and 7 show differentials in post-school outcomes for fifth-form school-leavers in the YCS and SELS cohorts. The tables continue some of the themes developed during the description of the Census of Population data. Looking at Table 6 first, participation in education and training is seen to increase for Catholics and Protestants at first destination between 1985 and 1992 whereas employment rates are observed to decrease. However, whilst there are absolute changes in the statuses of young people between 1985 and 1992 there are still differentials between Catholics and Protestants in terms of educational participation, training participation, and employment.

Table 6: 'First Destinations' in the YCS and SELS by Religion

| | YCS | | | SELS | | |
| | April 1985 | | | April 1992 | | |
Status	Catholic	Protestant	Difference (pp)	Catholic	Protestant	Difference (pp)
Education	29.6	26.7	2.9	37.4	34.2	3.2
Employment	30.9	42.7	-11.8	15.5	22.8	-7.3
Training	30.7	23.4	7.3	42.8	36.3	6.5
Unemployment/ other	8.7	7.2	1.5	4.5	6.7	-2.2
Number	479	765	-	348	421	-

Source: YCS and SELS

Table 7: 'Final Destinations' in the YCS and SELS by Religion

| | YCS | | | SELS | | |
| | October 1987 | | | October 1994 | | |
Status	Catholic	Protestant	Difference (pp)	Catholic	Protestant	Difference (pp)
Education	1.1	2.0	-0.9	18.3	15.0	3.3
Employment	66.3	77.9	-11.6	57.2	67.0	-9.8
Training	2.6	0.1	2.5	5.2	2.9	2.3
Unemployment/ other	30.0	20.0	10.0	19.3	15.1	4.2
Number	466	751	-	306	345	-

Source: YCS and SELS

For all statuses (with the exception of unemployment) the signs of the differentials remain relatively constant. Moving on to consider 'final destination' in Table 7, a similar pattern is observable. Catholics and Protestants, for example, both experienced a fall in employment rate of about 10pp but a Catholic/Protestant differential has been maintained. Another key point to note is that educational participation increased between 1987 and 1994 and that in line with data from the Census of Population Catholics have a higher rate of participation. It would be interesting to see how differentials later evolved but unfortunately the data on "later careers" are restricted to a "final destination" only some 2-3 years after leaving school.

Other analytical perspectives on Catholic/Protestant differentials

The analysis has so far concentrated upon observed Catholic/Protestant differentials as described by the Census of Population, the YCS and the SELS. The overall observation is that there is no evidence that observed religious differentials, particularly in terms of employment, have lessened. Furthermore, religious differentials in unemployment are still significant and new ones have also arisen in terms of training and education according to data from the YCS, SELS and the Census. These religious inequalities are apparent not only as differential participation rates but are also seen, for example, in the quality of training that young people can access (SACHR 1996).

Catholic/Protestant differentials might not be caused specifically by religion but could be due to *compositional effects* (Smith and Chambers 1991). It is well known, for example, that the Catholic and Protestant communities differ in their composition in educational background, family size, and parental socio-economic status. Lower Catholic average educational attainment, larger mean family size, and the greater likelihood that Catholics come from a household with a family experience of unemployment mean that Catholic young people might be forecast, for example, to have lower rates of employment than Protestants regardless of any specific and particular impact of religion.

To test whether religion has an independent effect on post-school outcomes preliminary analyses by Murphy and Shuttleworth (1997a, 1997b), controlled for the compositional influences of qualifications gained at school, type of school attended (whether a grammar school or a secondary school), number of siblings, parental labour market status and gender on post-school outcomes using the YCS and SELS. Qualifications gained at school were an important predictor of post-school outcome, increasing the chances of being in education whereas better qualifications meant that there was less chance of being in employment or training. Gender was significant in that males were more likely than females to participate in training and there were also some effects arising from parental labour market status and number of siblings.

An important result was that religion was, in many cases, a significant independent predictor of post-school outcomes at "first destination" after leaving school, and also at "final destination" even after other background variables had been taken into account. Catholic young people were less likely than Protestants, everything else being equal, to enter employment and were more likely to enter training or education. Overall, the general patterns suggest that there were few changes in the determinants of inequality between the YCS and SELS cohorts suggesting that post-school outcomes were structured by much the same factors in 1991 as in 1985 despite many changes in the labour market, in education and in training provision. The results also suggest that religion has some impact over and above those caused by measured compositional differences between the Catholic and Protestant communities. In other words, a young Catholic still has less likelihood of being in employment than a Protestant identical in terms of parents' labour market status, educational background, gender, and family size.

DISCUSSION

The analysis of the educational and economic statuses of young people suggests that not only have Catholic/Protestant differentials not been eradicated (although the complete removal of differentials might be impossible given 'compositional differences' between Catholics and Protestants) but that they have probably even increased for employment. Over the long term, consideration of Census of Population data shows that employment rates fell significantly between 1971 and 1991, educational participation rose, as did unemployment, but that Catholic/Protestant differentials remained stubbornly in place. Preliminary analyses of the YCS and SELS indicate that these interpretations of the Census data are robust and that the predictors of post-school outcome which were significant in 1985 (religion, gender, educational attainment, family background) remained important for 1991 school-leavers.

Labour market differentials amongst older people might be plausibly dismissed, at least in part, as relicts of processes occurring in the 1950s, 1960s and 1970s but the evidence presented suggests that they are, in fact, contemporary in their action as they are influencing young people in the 1980s and 1990s. Should this early post-school stage influence later life chances (see, for example, Breen 1991; Furlong 1992), then this implies that religious differentials might be a problem far into Northern Ireland's future.

At one level, these findings are remarkable. The Northern Ireland labour market has experienced many major changes since 1971 amongst which loom the loss of manual employment, the growth of service employment, feminisation of jobs, and declines in male economic activity. This process of restructuring has influenced all sections of the labour market, but its effects have been particularly marked for young people (Ashton et al 1990). Educational developments and the growth of training provision have added to these changes. The maintenance of religious differentials despite these significant transformations is therefore intriguing. In terms of the discussion outlined earlier in the chapter, the evidence from the Census data, YCS and SELS suggests that the increased number of post-school destinations, the new 'protracted transition', and the growth in educational participation have not equalised outcomes between Catholics and Protestants. It seems, as Furlong (1992) argues, that post-school outcomes for young people in the 1990s can be predicted with reference to the same factors as in the past.

Yet, at another level, the findings are unremarkable. The headline Catholic male unemployment rate has remained over twice as high as that for Protestant males since 1971 (Gudgin and Breen 1996; Murphy and Armstrong 1994) although the ratio of rates declined from 2.6 in the 1971 Census of Population to 2.2 in the 1991 Census of Population and to 2.1 in the 1993 Labour Force Survey. However, despite these fluctuations, the Catholic/Protestant unemployment ratio appears to be relatively stable and it had not fallen to 1.5 by 1995 as hoped by SACHR (1987). The persistence of the male Catholic/Protestant unemployment differential requires explanation. Gudgin and Breen (1996) point to one or more equilibriating mechanisms that maintain constancy in the male unemployment ratio and suggest as their candidates interactions between differential rates of Catholic/Protestant population growth, migration, job quit rates, and disadvantage in hiring. The single largest component identified by Gudgin and Breen (1996) is Catholic disadvantage in hiring but much public debate has emphasised greater rates of Catholic natural increase (and an unwillingness of Catholics to leave Northern Ireland) as significant causes of Catholic unemployment and the displacement of Protestants in jobs by Catholics. The findings presented in this chapter question this interpretation: migration probably has had little time to impact upon new school-leavers, the balance of disadvantage can plausibly be assumed to be less for young people than older people since members of the YCS and SELS sample had just exited the school system, and the reported analysis of the SELS (Murphy and Shuttleworth 1997a) outlines gender and social class differentials in post-school outcomes that imply specific social forces are important rather than general demographic effects. Demographic explanations of differentials in Northern Ireland possibly have some utility but they also need to be set in a wider international context which suggests that long-lasting labour market, social and educational differentials are not so unusual that they require analysts to invoke special equilibrating mechanisms. Against this background, differentials might be considered 'normal' if not acceptable outcomes of social stratification.

It is difficult to find a precise analogy for the demographic, social and political situation of Northern Ireland. However, a comparison that has commonly been made is with Black/White unemployment and income differentials in the United States. Here, the evidence suggests that unemployment differentials for both young people and adults have remained resistant to similar patterns of economic, institutional and social change as noted in Northern Ireland as well as the Civil Rights legislation of the 1960s. With reference to young people aged 18-24, Jencks (1992) observes that the black unemployment rate is about twice as high as the white rate and that both rates have risen together with a maintenance of the differential. Table 8 presents an alternative perspective on the issue presenting employment and unemployment rates between 1964 and 1986.

Table 8: Black/White Employment and Unemployment Differentials

Year	Black Unemployment	White Unemployment	Ratio	Black Employment	White Employment	Ratio
1964	7.7	3.1	2.48	77.7	82.2	0.94
1969	3.7	2.3	1.60	77.5	81.4	0.95
1975	11.7	6.2	1.88	77.1	80.7	0.96
1979	8.7	3.6	2.41	68.8	77.2	0.89
1984	13.0	5.7	2.28	65.6	74.5	0.88
1986	11.7	5.3	2.20	66.8	74.2	0.90

Source: Author's own calculations from Bound and Freeman (1989, p34)

There has been a general increase in unemployment, and a decrease in employment for both blacks and whites, but employment and unemployment differentials continue.

The ratio of unemployment rates in particular appears to have fluctuated more than the Catholic/Protestant male unemployment ratio in Northern Ireland, and the decline of the unemployment ratio below two in 1969 and 1975 is noteworthy. However, the fall was not consistent throughout the 1964-86 period and the evidence indicates an increase in the ratio during the 1980s which might be attributed to the impact of recession or the weakening of affirmative action (Bound and Freeman 1989).

Moving on from the description of labour market differentials to broader social and educational inequalities there is other evidence which indicates the entrenched nature of differentials. Shavit and Blossfeld (1993), reviewing evidence on inequalities in educational attainment and educational access from a variety of thirteen different countries over the long term conclude that the impact of socio-economic restructuring and educational reforms appear minimal as there is a great deal of stability in the relationship between socio-economic background and educational attainment. In six case studies (Germany, England, Hungary, Poland, Israeli Arabs) there is no evidence for change and in five (USA, Italy, Taiwan, Japan, Czechoslovakia) the evidence is mixed.

In this international context, the resistance of labour market and post-school outcome differentials to socio-economic restructuring and legislation in Northern Ireland do not appear to be startling since similar inequalities remain in the United States and other countries. The causes for the persistence of these differentials are unclear but in the United States structural factors that emphasise social processes, social control, and group forces and identification have been used as explanations (Shulman and Darity 1989). Similar explanations could also be valid in Northern Ireland particularly in the context of a divided society and the powerful influence of past social experiences on contemporary outcomes.

CONCLUSION

The persistence of labour market and post-school differentials in Northern Ireland, together with the evidence from the United States and other countries concerning labour market and educational differentials, could be used as a counsel of despair. Labour market differentials appear to be resistant to economic change, social developments, and legislation, and therefore probably incapable of solution. If this is so, why bother? In Northern Ireland the answer to this question lies in the political reality which means that the economic and political system has to be seen to be fair to both Catholics and Protestants, and in considerations of social justice. For the foreseeable future employment equality is therefore likely to be very much on the political agenda in Northern Ireland. This raises the issue of the most appropriate legislation to give the best chances of achieving the objective of reducing social and economic differentials. These questions also have a wider relevance beyond Northern Ireland since the 1976 and the 1989 Fair Employment Acts were informed, at least in part, by Canadian and United States employment equality practice.

To some extent, there is insufficient evidence from using the 1991 Census of Population, the YCS and SELS to make many comments about the success or failure of the 1989 Fair Employment Act. The FEC was only established in 1990 and its effects were unlikely to be felt by 1991. However, the 1976 Fair Employment Act does not seem to have closed observed Catholic/Protestant labour market differentials amongst young people - and numerous other policy interventions in the 1970s and 1980s do not seem to have reduced religious differentials in general post-school outcomes, nor the importance of family background and religion in structuring young peoples' destinations in work, training and education.

Moreover, the data presented in this chapter suggests that the 1989 Fair Employment Act has poor prospects for success in equalising post-school outcomes amongst young people. This is because fair employment legislation is still largely employment oriented and directed at employers' practices. For this reason, it will probably not be effective for young people (particularly those aged 16-19), because employment has declined in numerical importance for these age groups with the growth of education and training. This development is important for fair employment because early post-school destinations are important determinants of later labour market outcomes and future success in gaining employment. The emphasis on employment means that the key issues of education and training for young people are ignored by the FEC even though inequalities at this stage of life can have later employment repercussions.

Given the significance of early careers in structuring later life chances there is a strong case to be made for intervention in education and training at this early stage to ensure a more equitable foundation for careers. Many of the root causes of inequality appear to begin within the education system or to make themselves felt immediately on leaving school (or in the decision to 'stay-on' or to leave). Policy intervention for adults, although laudable, might therefore come too late since labour market and educational differentials may already be too deeply rooted to remove as they have been created during the school years or immediately after leaving school. Since social class and religion impact on educational outcomes within the Northern Ireland selective grammar/secondary school system, and then via education on post-school destinations (Shuttleworth 1994), a plausible argument might be made for early interventions to supplement the demand-side employer-driven 1989 Fair Employment Act.

In thinking about possible policies it is necessary to attempt to define the causes of Catholic/Protestant differentials. The preliminary analyses of Murphy and Shuttleworth (1997a, 1997b) indicate that the observed Catholic/Protestant post-school differentials consist of a *compositional* portion (structural differences between Catholics and Protestants in education, family size and family background) and a portion that is associated with the independent effect of *religion*. The meaning of this effect is disputed. It could be caused by religion, or perhaps by some other unknown variable correlated with religion. In either case the outcome, if Catholic disadvantage, is the same. Given these considerations, possible policies might take, as a first stage, the targeting of social need within schools and households to reduce educational and social differentials. This would address so-called structural Catholic/Protestant differences. A second stage of policy would be intervention during the first years after leaving school as a form of outreach to young Catholics to attack the independent effect of religion. More careers advice might be a good starting point as a way to offer guidance during the important first post-school years, but other interventions to ensure equal access to good quality training and education are also important given the Catholic/Protestant training differentials identified by SACHR (1996). In combination these, or similar measures, suggest a proactive series of educational, training, careers guidance, and labour market initiatives to manage post-school outcomes in such a way as to minimise differentials later in life. This potentially offers a realistic opportunity to reduce Catholic/Protestant differentials in the future.

REFERENCES

Ashton, D., Maguire, M., Spilsbury, M., (1990), *Restructuring the Labour Market: The Implications for Youth*, Macmillan, London

Bell, D. (1973), *The Coming of Post-Industrial Society*, Basic Books, New York

Bound, J., Freeman, R., (1989), Black economic progress: erosion of post-1965 gains in the 1980s?, in Shulman, S., Darity, W., (eds), *The Question of Discrimination: Racial Inequality in the US Labor Market*, Wesleyan University Press, Middletown, Connecticut, 33-49

Breen, R. (1991), *Education, Employment and Training in the Youth Labour Market*, ESRI Paper 152, Dublin

Cormack, R., Osborne, R., Thompson, W., (1980), *Into Work? Young School-Leavers and the Structure of Opportunity in Belfast*, Fair Employment Agency, Belfast

Cormack, R., Osborne, R., (eds.), *Discrimination and Public Policy in Northern Ireland*, Clarendon Press, Oxford

Furlong, A. (1992), *Growing up in a Classless Society? School to Work Transitions*, Edinburgh University Press, Edinburgh

Gertler. M. (1988), The limits to flexibility: comments on the Post-Fordist vision of production and its geography, *Transactions of the Institute of British Geographers New Series*, 13(4), 419-432

Gudgin, G., Breen, R., (1996), *Evaluation of the Ratio of Unemployment Rates as an Indicator of Fair Employment*, Central Community Relations Unit Employment Equality Research Paper 4, Belfast

Hart, P. (1988), *Youth Unemployment in Great Britain*, NIESR and Cambridge University Press, Cambridge

Jencks, C., (1992), *Rethinking Social Policy: Race, Poverty and the Underclass*, Harvard University Press, Cambridge, Massachusetts

McGarry, J., O'Leary, B., (1995), *Explaining Northern Ireland: Broken Images*, Blackwell, Oxford

McWhirter, L. (1989), Longitudinal evidence on the teenage years, in Harbison, J. (ed.), *Growing Up in Northern Ireland*, Learning Resources Unit, Stranmillis College, Belfast, 66-92

Metcalf, H., (1996), The Fair Employment Commission as a regulatory and enforcement agency, in McVey, J., Hutson, N., (eds), *Public Views and Experiences of Fair Employment and Equality Issues in Northern Ireland*, SACHR, Belfast, 145-167

Murphy, A., Armstrong, D., (1994), *A Picture of the Catholic and Protestant Male Unemployed*, Central Community Relations Unit Employment Equality Review Research Report 2, Belfast

Murphy, A., Shuttleworth, I., (1997a), Education, religion and the "first destinations" of recent school-leavers in Northern Ireland, *Economic and Social Review*, 28 (1), 23-41

Murphy, A., Shuttleworth, I., (1997b), *Religion, "First Destinations" and Later Careers: Evidence from the 1980s and 1990s in Northern Ireland*, unpublished paper, ILM Conference, Understanding the School-to-Work Transition, Robert Gordon University, Aberdeen, June 16th-17th

Payne, J. (1995), *Qualifications Between 16 and 18: A Comparison of Achievements on Routes Beyond Compulsory Schooling*, Employment Department Research Series Youth Cohort Report 32, Policy Studies Institute, London

Roberts, K., Clark, S., Wallace, C., (1994), Flexibility and individualisation: a comparison of transitions into employment in England and Germany, *Sociology*, 28 (1), 31-54

Rose, S., Magill, D., (1996), The development of fair employment legislation in Northern Ireland, in Magill, D., Rose, S., (eds), *Fair Employment Law in Northern Ireland: Debates and Issues*, SACHR, Belfast, 1-25

Shavit, Y., Blossfeld, H-P., (1993), *Persistent Inequality: Changing Educational Attainment in Thirteen Countries*, Westview Press, Boulder, Colorado

Shulman, S., Darity, W., (eds), *The Question of Discrimination: Racial Inequality in the US Labor Market*, Wesleyan University Press, Middletown, Connecticut

Shuttleworth, I. (1994), *An Analysis of Community Differences in the Pilot Northern Ireland Secondary Education Leavers' Survey*, Central Community Relations Unit Research Paper 3, Belfast

Smith, D., Chambers, G. (1991), *Inequality in Northern Ireland*, Clarendon Press, Oxford

Smyth, J., Cebulla, A. (1995) Industrial collapse and the post-fordist overdetermination of Belfast in P. Shirlow (ed.) *Development Ireland*, Pluto, London, 81-93

SACHR, (1987), *Religious and Political Discrimination and Equality of Opportunity in Northern Ireland*, Cm 237, HMSO, London

SACHR, (1996), *Employment Equality; Building for the Future*, Cm 3684, HMSO, London

INDEX